Tyndale House Publishers, Inc.
Carol Stream, Illinois

Ryan Dobson ↔ Toben Heim

Wrecked

What God can do when things crash and burn

Visit Tyndale's exciting Web site at www.tyndale.com

For more information about Ryan Dobson's KOR ministry, visit www.KORWorldMinistries.com

TYNDALE and Tyndale's quill logo are registered trademarks of Tyndale House Publishers, Inc.

Wrecked: What God Can Do When Things Crash and Burn

Designed by Ron Kaufmann

Edited by Stephanie Voiland and Brian Smith

Library of Congress Cataloging-in-Publication Data

Dobson, Ryan.
  Wrecked : what God can do when things crash and burn / Ryan Dobson and Toben Heim.
    p. cm.
  ISBN-13: 978-1-4143-1709-0 (sc)
  ISBN-10: 1-4143-1709-3 (sc)
  1. God (Christianity)—Omnipotence. 2. Providence and government of God—Christianity. 3. Consolation. 4. Spiritual formation. I. Heim, Toben, date. II. Title.
  BT133.D63 2007
  248.8'6 dc22   2007023396

Printed in the United States of America

14 13 12 11 10 09 08
7 6 5 4 3 2 1

We have come across dozens of people in our years of ministry who have shared their stories with us, many of whom appear in part in this book. However, we have done our best to change key details to make these people unrecognizable—their stories are theirs to tell, and we do not want to overstep those boundaries in this book. In other places we have combined elements of similar stories for the sake of making a more concise point. Please take the stories, all of which have a basis in truth, as they were intended—as opportunities for growth, as they have been for us.

Throughout my life, in the good times
and the bad times, there have been many people who have
stood by my side and supported me, but none more
than my parents. Mom and Dad, this book
is dedicated to you. Without your guidance, advice,
wisdom, and prayers I wouldn't be the man I am today.
I hope I'm making you proud. Thank you so much.

—R. D.

To Joanne, who has stuck with me through
thick and thin . . . and really thin.

—T. H.

Contents

CHAPTER 1: Feeling Wrecked?...1

CHAPTER 2: What Culture Says about the Wrecked Life..............15

CHAPTER 3: Oh Church, Where Art Thou?...................................41

CHAPTER 4: The Wrecked Life: Disobedience...........................67

CHAPTER 5: The Wrecked Life: Circumstance 93

CHAPTER 6: The Wrecked Life: Obedience 123

CHAPTER 7: Out of the Fish's Belly... 157

Acknowledgments 175

About the Authors.. 177

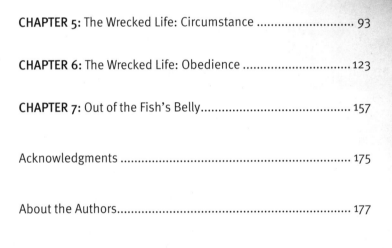

Feeling Wrecked?

— — —

If anyone knows what it's like to be wrecked, it's us.
Between the two of us we've been through a life-
threatening illness (including a month spent in the
hospital), financial stress, relational failures, the loss of
a job, the unexpected loss of a loved one, struggles with
acute materialism, clinical depression, bipolar disorder,
alcoholism, and divorce.

Somewhere in your gut, you probably have a pretty
good idea what it looks like—and feels like—to be
wrecked. Chances are you've been wrecked at some point
in the past. You might be standing, sitting, or sprawling in
the middle of your life's wreckage right now. And unfortunately, you'll most likely have a wreck or five in the future.
You're surrounded, too, by thousands of other people who

are at this very moment completely, utterly, and hopelessly wrecked. Whether they show it on the outside or not.

Have you ever been in a car wreck? Living in Colorado, we both have spent our share of time driving on icy roads. We've both been in car accidents. (No, not serious ones, thankfully. But enough to know that gut-tearing feeling when you see another car veer into your lane.)

Or when you slam on the brakes because the car you were following too closely comes to an instant dead stop.

Or when you realize you cut the corner too tight, too fast, and your tires lose traction.

And you start to slide.

In those seconds you feel absolutely helpless. Completely out of control. Something bad is about to happen, and you can't stop it. It's *going* to happen. Time is suspended. The seconds stretch on. Your thoughts race. You're about to lose your lunch.

You brace for impact.

You pray.

You scream.

Then impact.

Watching yourself slide helplessly toward a life wreck can have that same sense of inevitability. Your adrenaline spikes, and all you can do is cover your face. And you know: This is going to hurt.

Death, taxes, and wrecks. Life guarantees them all. And it's not like chicken pox—down once and safe forever. No one is immune to fresh disaster. That's a tough pill to swallow, because a lot of us, especially Christians, have created a fantasy reality where if we stay "inside God's will" and make all the right choices, we'll somehow avoid life's really big smackdowns.

Nice try. But it won't happen.

Want proof? Pick up your Bible and try to find one individual who loved God and was loved by God who didn't go through some seriously tough times. Go to the New Testament, the Old Testament—it doesn't matter. Everywhere you look, you'll find people who did everything right and still got squeezed through some agonizing wringer.

Your own circle of friends and family is proof. Look carefully. Can you find that one person who has somehow made it past twenty without heartache? Some people may look like they have it all together, like unscathed survivors. But the scars are there. You see them when you get to know their hearts, when their defenses drop and they tell their stories . . . the real stories.

The more people you meet, the firmer your realization: No one gets a wreck-free life.

Now finally, take a look at your own life. Pain is part of the human experience. It's built in, a standard feature. Comes with the package, whether you ask for it or not. It stems from something that happened at the very beginning with a couple of your relatives—Adam and Eve. They blew it for all of us. (Of course, we would have, too. So don't hate them.)

We can be wrecked in a bunch of different ways, but they all boil down to three basic flavors: wreckage from sin, wreckage from circumstances, and—ready for this?—wreckage from *obedience*.

Of course, we expect bad fruit from the first category, when we make wrong choices, when we sin. Habitual speeders are crashes (or tickets) waiting to happen. Are we shocked when the inevitable comes down? Probably not. Disappointed, angry . . . but not surprised.

Now, we may not like the second category, but we know that circumstances can wreck us too. Look around at events of the past few years in places like Southeast Asia and New Orleans. Tsunamis and Katrinas. We know that uncontrollable circumstances can take us down. Closer to home, divorce hurts kids who had nothing to do with the problem. Addiction robs innocent families of moms and dads, sons and daughters. Sickness and accidents rip loved ones from our arms. Circumstances sometimes seem to hunt us down, conspiring to wreck us.

The third category is less obvious. It's not a popular message, inside or outside church walls, that *doing the right thing* can totally wreck us. But this truth couldn't be more obvious in Scripture. Doing what God calls us to do doesn't guarantee an easy, carefree life. In fact, it usually promises just the opposite. According to tradition, ten of Jesus' disciples—the venerable founders of Christianity—were executed. Hebrews 11 is a catalog of godly people who, through the ages, suffered every kind of hardship imaginable. Persecution, destitution, starvation, homelessness, prison, beating, stoning, torture, murder.

Matthew 7:13-14 says this: "Enter through the narrow gate. For wide is the gate and broad is the road that leads to destruction, and many enter through it. But small is the gate and narrow the road that leads to life, and only a few find it."

The wide path. The easy route. Going with the crowd, drifting with the current. Lots of opportunities to blow it, to sin, to be hurt by other people's sins. It's simple math: Regular exposure to sin behaviors—yours or others'—is a spawning ground for tragedy.

But avoiding wreckage isn't easy. It would be nice if following the narrow path, the path that Christ calls us to, guaranteed we wouldn't get hurt. But here's the thing: We'll get wrecked in some way no matter what path we follow. Obedience isn't a bulletproof vest. The "armor of God" in Ephesians 6—you know, truth, righteousness, faith . . . all the rest—protects us from sin, not from pain and loss. In fact, Jesus promised that we'd suffer *because* of our obedience.

Wreckage happens. And theories that sound nice on paper evaporate when it happens to you.

Being truly wrecked isn't about being annoyed or inconvenienced. Or about getting your feathers ruffled. It's not the missing car keys; you can replace them. Or the test you flunked; you can take the class again. Or the argument with your best friend; you can make up.

Being wrecked means reaching that point where you see no way out. Period. It's when the little light that was at the end of the tunnel goes dark. It's fear and hopelessness and helplessness. It's wanting to give up, concede total failure in life, cash it in for good.

[Toben] *My wife, Joanne, has been there. And I was the cause. I was right in the middle of discovering my bipolar disorder, and I was ineptly trying to self-medicate with alcohol. Our marriage was a disaster. I was no kind of husband. I was ignoring my family.*

Joanne got a lot of advice from different people. Fortunately some counseled her to hang on. But others advised the opposite. In the darkness of that time, there were some who saw the situation as so bleak that she should give me the boot and file for divorce. That would have been the easier way for her to go. But in that darkness, she chose to wait it out.

Most of us know that dark place. We see no exit signs. The good options seem to have disappeared, and the ones that remain, if we're left with any choice, guarantee only grief. That's being wrecked.

Maybe you're wrecked in a way that's apparent only to you. No one else sees your struggle. You're having a hard time controlling your thoughts; your mind wanders—or lunges—to places you wish it wouldn't go, and you can't see any mental off-ramps. You, like the apostle Paul, "have the desire to do what is good, but . . . cannot carry it out" (Romans 7:18).

Or maybe you're feeling nostalgic for an old, abandoned sin—something you've tried to put behind you but that still has a hold on you. "How your body still remembers things you told it to forget. How those furious affections followed you." Does that line from the Weakerthans' song "Watermark" describe you?

Or maybe anxiety has your number—pervasive worry, dread, depression. You feel utterly isolated. You can't get outside your own head. No one knows, so they can't help. Your inner wreckage is sucking you into a void.

[Toben] *This is familiar territory for me. I've wrestled with depression, anxiety, and bipolar disorder for years. It wrecked me for years before I began to deal with it. I had sunk so deep into that abyss that by the time I got help it took me two years and untold thousands of dollars for counseling and medication to get out. I felt like no one around me knew how to help. And I didn't know how to ask.*

On the other hand, maybe your wreck is public. Debris from your life is strewn out in plain view, rubble scattered along the highway. At rush hour. Everyone's gawking, whispering.

A divorce. A destructive relationship. An addictive habit that, to your horror, bobbed up to the surface.

Struggles with your job. Failure with your finances. Or any number of other humiliating revelations.

You want people to think you've got it all together. We all do. And when they see that you don't, the shame can be suffocating. Everyone has advice: Where you went wrong. How you should fix it. You want to do something, but you don't even know where to begin.

What if there was a way to redeem this bad stuff? To turn it into something good. Too good to be true? Good question. We'll talk more about this later.

[Ryan] *I got so tired of hearing "God is doing this for a reason" while I was going through my divorce. As if God caused my divorce, and somehow that was supposed to make me feel better. Why? Well, He's God, right? And He's supposedly using the pain to prepare me for something great later in life.*

Whatever, *I thought cynically.* If it's all right with You, I'll just have my marriage back, thanks.

God didn't cause my divorce. He did allow it to happen as a result of our choices and disobedience. And in His grace He miraculously used it to steer me back on track. (More on that later.)

Maybe your wreck feels an awful lot like being stuck. You're at a dead standstill, paralyzed, unable to get going again. People ask how you are, and you reply fine, thanks—knowing you're far from fine. But you can't even buy a clue as to why.

[Ryan] *I can remember sitting on my couch watching TV several years ago during the worst season of my life. I was sleeping about fifteen hours a day and watching TV all the other hours. I'd quit my job, had no other source of income, and couldn't have cared less. I was on the brink of losing my house. So what? Everything else was gone. Why worry about a house?*

I couldn't see any way out. I'd tried to find one, but after a while I just stopped looking.

Now, it's possible that you're in a rather obscure subset of people: followers of Jesus who actually listen to Him. People who honestly follow Him—in what you *do*, not just in your words and rituals.

And you're wrecked.

You've chosen a path completely outside the norm, a path that you believe God has called you to. You're faithfully walking that path, and your life is anything but rosy. Maybe your family thinks you're nuts, or maybe you can't make ends meet. Maybe when you're alone and quiet, you wonder if you really heard God right or if you misunderstood and made a really bad decision somewhere along the way.

You look for affirmation from God, but a lot of the time you just don't feel it. You poured your life into this calling. So why are things so hard? You play out a script each day, talking yourself into faith, persistence, another twenty-four hours of what you hope is obedience. And you're afraid that one day you'll forget the script. Then who knows what will happen.

[Ryan] *I ignored God's calling on my life when I first heard it. I felt the call to speak and preach God's message, but I was tired of living hand to mouth. All my friends were getting "real" jobs with steady paychecks. I was getting whatever people decided to pay me. As much as I loved it and felt it was my calling, I turned my back on speaking in exchange for a dream of security that never came true. In fact, I was never more miserable than when I was working a steady job. I knew it wasn't what God had called me to.*

I'm nowhere close to perfect now, but I am in the middle of God's will. I know it. I love it.

And the wreckage goes on.

A Promise

Cheer up! That's right, you *will* be wrecked in your lifetime, probably many times, and for any or all of the reasons we've mentioned. Every time, it will hurt like hell—in the true meaning of that word. And in those terrifying moments, in those bleakest of circumstances, God can do something very good. He can teach us about ourselves. And about Him.

Whatever your situation—whether you're wrecked by sin, by life in general, or by obedience—don't give up hope. You're not alone. God is there. And all of us know what it's like to feel somewhere between a little roughed up and totally devastated. All of us know that stuck feeling, when we don't seem to have the capacity to break out and move forward.

Each of us has a unique pain history. But although our stories vary from yours in the particulars, the bottom-line emotional themes are common to all humanity. So when God sets a gift in front of us—other people who can tell their stories—we listen, find comfort, and learn.

This is a journey we need to take together.

This book is about two things: first, leaning into and learning from our wrecked times, no matter what causes them; and second, allowing ourselves to be wrecked in a whole new way—in a redeemed way—by a God who loves us too much to let us live forever in a safe, boring comfort zone.

Sounds crazy. We know. But stick with us.

For most of us, this is strange new territory. No one prepared us for the wrecked life. And when it happens, everyone has their own Band-Aids to stick on it. Some say, "Numb out to the pain." Others say, "Just have all the fun you can." Even the church doesn't always know how to deal with wrecked people.

Yet somehow God can use our tough times to change us, to make us more like Christ. That's why, amazingly, He actually calls us to lives of wrecked obedience.

Rest assured, we know what we're talking about. This isn't just theory for us. We've lived it.

Why Us?

Maybe you're wondering why a couple of fairly normal guys decided to tackle this topic. For starters, it's something we feel called to. God put it on our minds. It's been stuck there, and He won't let us forget about it. For the six years we've known each other, our conversations, when we're not talking about surfing or skating, have often turned to this topic. Sometimes it's because we're aware of wreckage we see in someone else's life. But just as often we're in the middle of some wreckage of our own. We've been through some real ups and downs together, and this book is the outgrowth of those late-night sessions in the kitchen over coffee when we just opened up and let the pieces of scrap metal fly!

[Ryan] *A friend introduced Toben and me at dinner one night. I was going through my divorce and was just starting to hear God's voice again. In my pain and bitterness, I had blocked it out for a long time. As the night wore on and people started leaving, Tob and I stayed up talking. I don't know why, but I opened up to him and told him my story. I was hurting and he was listening.*

I arrived that night a stranger and left with a friend. I tell people Toben is the brother I never had. I know he'd take a bullet for me, and he also tells me when I'm wrong. I may not like it, but knowing he loves me and has my best interests at heart, I can take it. I'm a better person for having Tob in my life.

You'll hear more details of our stories as we go, but suffice it to say that we have been, currently are, and expect in the future to be, a couple of wrecked guys. We've been wrecked by our own sin and disobedience, wrecked by some really lousy circumstances, and wrecked by doing what God called us to. And we've had the good fortune to have experienced a lot of this stuff together. We've been mirrors to each other, helping each other see ourselves and our motives honestly, reflecting back and forth the lessons we've learned in wreckage school.

Throughout the book we'll tell you lots of stories, most of them about us, and some of them ugly. Why? Because we know what it is to walk the wide path that leads to destruction and carnage. Sometimes people romanticize wreckage and think, *Man, those folks on the wide path seem to be having so much fun. I wish I could do that.* But if you look more closely, you'll see a mess. We know. At times, that mess has been us.

We also want to share with you what we've learned about being wrecked by obedience. We still have a lot we don't understand, and neither of us is immune to making unwise decisions again. But we do know a few things for sure, like the value of walking into wreckage when God says to. We also know that God, in His grace, may give us times of relative peace and quiet. We're incredibly thankful for those, but we guard against believing we're entitled to them.

We like to think of the wrecked life in terms of this

mental image: God puts things into our hands and takes things out as well. If we keep our hands open to Him, He's free to do both easily. But if we clench our fists around the stuff He has temporarily given us, He may have to break our fingers when it comes time to take it out.

We're a couple of wrecked guys who are trying to live that openhanded life, ready for whatever God throws our way. We don't have it all figured out, but we desire to live the best kind of life God wants for us. And from our experiences, that's an attitude God can work with.

What Culture Says about the Wrecked Life

— — —

[Toben] *My wife and I grew up in "comfortable" families—not too rich but certainly not lacking for much. As newlyweds we weren't living the comfortable life we were accustomed to. We were both college students working part-time jobs, trying to make ends meet. Most of the time the meeting of the ends came by way of the shiny gold Visa card that had been so easy to obtain.*

"Making ends meet" meant something different for us than it typically meant for previous generations. It required the latest clothes, new shoes, dinners out, vacations, and just about anything else we "needed." Looking back, we didn't really need any of that stuff, and we certainly didn't need the nearly $20,000 in debt that we racked up in our early twenties.

We thought we were entitled to live the way our parents lived, even though we hadn't earned the right (or the means) to live that way. We wanted our American dream to come true whether or not we had the money to pay for it.

Our American dream was borrowed.

Ah, the American dream! The house with the white picket fence, the Mercedes, the perfect little boy and the sweetest little girl, the rewarding career, the secure retirement. And for our generation, it goes even beyond this. We want freedom, status, approval, good looks, a great wardrobe, and the coolest technology. In some form or another, we all want to control our own destinies and create a good life through our own efforts.

The dream is deeply rooted in us because it's deeply rooted in the American psyche. We're all infected, and at some level it drives us in ways we're not even conscious of. To be fair, the American dream comes from noble roots. Honest, hardworking people who came to the United States to find a better way of life. Millions of people for centuries—and even still today—have sacrificed much and taken great risks because of the dream's allure.

Unfortunately, this allure is at the root of American materialism and consumerism, which has played a huge role in the last several decades in the corruption and disintegration of our culture. Our thing-obsession is a powerful influence. It has changed our basic assumptions about life. We now measure our whole life's success by our material success.

Now, we want to clarify: We don't believe wealth and possessions are bad in themselves. They can be gifts from God for our enjoyment. But when we shape our lives around the gift instead of the Giver, we've become materialistic. And that's when it turns bad.

And nothing is inherently wrong with the American dream . . . except this: We believe we're *entitled* to it. If we don't, for whatever reason, obtain it, then either something is wrong with us, or our circumstances have conspired against us.

This idea of entitlement is one of the many ways our culture warps our thinking about the wrecked life. We can be living a good life, with adequate provision, healthy relationships, and plenty of opportunity for personal fulfillment . . . and our culture-conditioned thinking says, "It's not enough." Instantly we're dissatisfied. And we scramble to improve our situation with blazing speed.

The necessities of life haven't changed. But maybe our hearts have. And in our frantic efforts to avoid the world's version of wreckage, we drive ourselves into real wreckage. We look at the people around us and think we need to upgrade to keep up. Or the constant torrent of advertising convinces us that new stuff will make us happy. The standards for what we "need" keep going up, and contentment seems harder and harder to come by. Maybe that's why the average person will have so many different careers over their lifetime (seven, on average). We all want more, and we want it now.

[Ryan] *I totally fell into this trap in my late twenties. A lot of my friends were buying houses, but I was still living in an apartment. Looking back, it was a pretty great place—quiet and comfortable, and more important, close to the beach. But I wasn't satisfied. If my friends were buying houses, why couldn't I? The answer: My job and my bank account were still only apartment-sized.*

I ignored those facts and bought a house anyway. I quickly got into more debt than I ever imagined possible. I was financially wrecked for almost six years, but I finally crawled out from under the debt and paid it off. But don't think for a second it hasn't crossed my mind to jump into a similar situation again. As much as I hate to admit it, culture speaks to me, too. When my friends buy new anything, part of me is actually convinced that I'm inadequate, or a failure—in other words, wrecked—unless I get one, too.

What culture promises, I think, is happiness. If we buy [fill-in-the-blank] we'll have the respect of our friends, we'll have status, we'll feel better about ourselves. That's why I fell into the trap—I felt inferior to the people around me, and I felt entitled to their status. So in some ways, I guess the struggle against culture really is more about a struggle against myself—trying to reconcile God's truth, which I say I believe, with worldly "truth," which I've actually bought into. The two are irreconcilable. To the degree that my godly thinking wins, the world believes I'm being wrecked. To the degree that my worldly thinking wins, I'm really wrecked.

We've opened this chapter by camping on materialism as one lie our culture tells us about the wrecked life. But culture has a way of taking virtually *any* good thing—designed by God for our benefit—and twisting it into an ugly force in our lives. Growing up in this culture, none of us can completely avoid being brainwashed to some extent. We're surrounded by the world's propaganda, which is reinforced constantly by media, magazines, music, government, friends, and family . . . and sometimes even by misguided fellow Christ followers and church leaders. When we look at our lives through cultural lenses, we see a distorted image of good things and we can mistreat and misuse them . . . to our destruction.

One obvious value that culture has twisted is sexuality. When we view our bodies and other people's bodies through the lens of secular culture, we see, not persons in God's image, but just bodies that we're entitled to use in whatever way makes us feel good. Promiscuity is practically a cultural mandate.

Many subtler twists on reality can lead to ruination if we let culture dictate our thinking. What about vanity, the constant obsession and pressure to look a particular way? Of course, it's good to be healthy, to exercise and take care of our bodies. But many people become totally consumed by a compulsion with appearance. Some are addicted to working out, and some literally starve themselves in pursuit of a particular weight or body type. Some fill their bodies with all sorts of dangerous drugs to achieve a culturally idealized body. They do this at their own peril.

What about the cultural messages about authority that we take in through media and entertainment? Without realizing it, we can be sucked into the subversive worldviews and values promoted by certain music and movies, and our thinking gradually becomes polluted with resentment and rebellion that spills over into our relationship with God.

Culture's lies can easily, cunningly skew our views of self, work, relationships, truth, and countless other aspects of this life. Any time we buy into what culture, not Christ, says, we step onto a conveyor belt that leads to some scary places.

A Rant

If you fail to live according to culture's ideals, on purpose or by accident, you're made to feel as though something's wrong with you. If you've rejected the idea that you need more money and a bigger house and a nicer car, then you're an outsider who doesn't fit in because you can't be marketed to. If you've rejected the idea that being a self-actualized person means having sex whenever you want, with whomever you want, then you're viewed as mentally ill or genetically deficient. If you don't buy the idea that a perfect body is the ultimate goal in life, then you'll only get curious nods (to your face) and mocking sneers (behind your back) from the hard-core gym crowd.

And if you don't go out there and claim everything you're simply entitled to, you're a wimp who has no self-respect. You deserve all the best. Just because.

[Ryan] *As part of Gen X, I've always hated the label Slacker Generation. But at times I have to admit there's some truth to it, and on a personal level, I'm sometimes the example that proves the label. I'd like to say I used to be that way, but the truth is, sometimes I still am.*

My generation's culture says I'm entitled to greatness just because I was born. I deserve that promotion, that raise, that recognition—not because of hard work, innovation, or excellence, but because I showed up.

But when it comes down to it, I'm not entitled to any of those things. I'm part of the "all" in "all have sinned and fall short of the glory of God."[1] What I'm entitled to is death and an eternity spent in hell. And what I need to strive for is excellence . . . not to prove my identity or to earn people's approval but because the Lord who loves me and died for me asked me to do it. It's right because it's for Him and because it will pay off in the end, for His glory.

Culture also says: If you don't base your whole identity on a romantic relationship, what could you possibly be worth?

We know a young woman—we'll call her Ellen—who

21

---

dated the same guy—we'll call him Wayne—for seven years. That's right, seven years! This relationship started their freshman year of college. A couple of years into this relationship, Ellen made the assumption, and reasonably so, that they would eventually be married. She and Wayne loved each other very much, enjoyed being together, were best friends, and had years of shared experiences under their belts.

Two more years went by, and she came to expect a proposal during their senior year, with a wedding planned for just after graduation. But senior year came and went without a proposal.

Now, Ellen and Wayne never actually talked about marriage. Ellen was afraid to freak him out or make him feel pressured.

And he just never brought it up.

By this point, Ellen's identity had become inextricably linked to this relationship. She'd accepted her culture's lie that she had no identity as a singular person; she, as a person, only had meaning as part of a couple who did couple things and hung out with other couples. Their friends began to get engaged and married, and her identity began to suffer. She began to suspect what she'd feared all along—she was defective.

But she hung in there. "Desperately clung on" might be a better way of saying it. She reasoned—*prayed*—that once she and Wayne got jobs and settled into postcollegiate life, her day would come. Time passed, and Ellen's personality started to change. She had been a joyful and vibrant person, but she became increasingly depressed and discouraged. She worried constantly that her greatest dream—her only dream—wasn't going to materialize. And somewhere along the way, she started slipping into deep codependency: Her happiness was dictated by Wayne's happiness and behavior.

You can probably guess how this ends. Three full years after college, Wayne got a job in another city and moved away. That's when he decided to finally end things with Ellen. Only one word describes her state in the months after he left . . . devastated. She cried constantly and couldn't pull herself together.

Heartbreak is one thing, and Ellen had every reason to experience it. But more than just her heart had been broken. Ellen had pinned her entire identity and future happiness on her relationship with this guy. She couldn't imagine life without him. He was at the center of her every daydream. When he walked away, she was wrecked to her very core. Her identity had long ago been absorbed into Wayne, and now she had no idea who she was, why she had any right to exist. She felt she'd never be happy again.

We've all believed some lie the world tells us about how to be happy, whether it's pinning our happiness on another person or an accomplishment or a posses-sion—some little god other than God. Inevitably, in some form or another, that idol will let us down. We discover that we've been basing our happiness on something very slippery. And yet we have a *horribly* hard time breaking out of the brainwashing, even after we've been wrecked. Culture keeps us dissatisfied with God's totally satisfying provision. The world lures us into trying the same old panacea for our new pain. Or maybe a fresh, new panacea for some very old pain.

This invisible battle is so hard that we need to remind ourselves daily . . . our happiness and our identity have to be pinned to something solid—namely, Christ, and who we are in Christ. He's our only hope for true joy. As long as our happiness is tied up in anything or anyone else, we will always end up disappointed and disillusioned. True happiness results when we change our mind-set and become thankful for and satisfied with God's provision for our real needs.

The world tantalizes us with happiness; God promises true joy. When we chase after "treasures in heaven" (see Matthew 6:19-20), we're on our way to real contentment and fulfillment.

Getting Sucked In

We'd be less than truthful if we left the impression that we've cast all the cultural lies aside to take a nobler path. Both of us have our embarrassing—and cataclysmic—episodes when we've pursued culture's empty promises, and you'll see examples of our misguided thinking as we tell our stories throughout this book. Here's one . . .

[Toben] *I took the summer off this year. You know . . . between jobs . . . Okay, I was unemployed.*

I'd saved up just enough money to take a full two months off. I'd never had more than a two-week vacation. Two months felt decadent. And what did I intend to do? Besides spending as much time with my family as possible, I intended to golf. A lot. I was convinced that the good life would come when I got to spend time every day on the course.

For the first few weeks I was in heaven. My game was improving, and I thought, I could really get used to living this way.

But then it got hot. I'd come back from the course tired and dehydrated and in serious need of a shower. And to be honest, the routine was starting to bore me. How many balls does one person need to hit? How many holes of golf a week really makes sense? So I skipped a day. And then another. And another.

And then my culture-bred fantasy dissolved. The thing I'd imagined would bring me the greatest satisfaction simply stopped delivering. But more than that, I realized that I'd wrapped up much of my identity in my "Toben as golfer" image. My awakening to reality caused a small identity crisis. I actually felt guilty for not going to the course. I found myself trading in my polo shirts for T-shirts and my golf slacks for cargo shorts. I morphed.

God is an amazing Teacher. In His grace, He allows me to run with my faulty thinking for a time, so I can see for myself why He has warned me against certain things in the Bible. And then He eventually brings me back to the way He would have me live.

Playing golf is not a sin. But pinning my happiness on golf isn't exactly God's path to my fulfillment. As I grew dissatisfied, God nudged me little by little toward His sources of true joy—Him first of all, and then the valuable relationships He has given me. I can imagine Him saying, "Ah, you've finally come around. Feels pretty good, doesn't it?" He's right. It feels great.

Relationships—the most important treasures any of us have on earth—are sometimes the victims of our cultural brainwashing. We think we have to live in a particular setting in order to have status and fulfillment, but if that comes at the expense of our families and friendships, these relationships wilt before our eyes. We seek fulfillment in the high-speed, high-need lifestyle, when our relationships may need something a little slower and saner that gives us more quality time together.

Many of us struggle with cognitive dissonance, saying we value people but spending time, money, and energy on the counterfeits we've been conned into valuing more. Thank God that He steps in and shakes up our priorities. He digs down and roots out the world's delusions and plants in their place *His* dreams.

And here is the real irony: Although culture's lies promise to free us from our pain, they do more to accentuate our wreckedness than to alleviate it. This shouldn't surprise followers of Christ. The Bible is clear that the pursuit of the world, and the values of the world, leads to emptiness (see 1 John 2:15-17). The pursuit of God, and the values of God, leads to genuine, eternal fulfillment.

Culture on the Wrecked Life

Culture's message about the wrecked life is short and sweet: You don't *need* to be wrecked . . . ever! But most of us end up wrecked at some point, no matter whose advice we follow. We might even know ahead of time that wreckedness is inevitable, but we certainly know it when the disaster strikes. This puts us at strange odds with our culture, doesn't it? We know our reality—we're broken—but we're still bombarded from every direction with assurances that we don't need to feel that way. After all, the American dream (or fill in any of the other lies) is all about success and satisfaction and feeling good. Even as the fantasies are fading before our eyes, culture keeps on telling us that they're the answer, that we have no reason to be wrecked.

Wrecked because of bad decisions? The world is there to offer a quick way out. Unwanted pregnancy? There's an "easy" solution: abortion—or easier yet, the abortion pill RU-486. Not happy in your marriage? Divorce proceedings are now quicker and more friendly than ever. You've overspent and you're short on funds? Just charge it to your credit card.

Our culture's feel-good consumerism is a multibillion-dollar industry. Magazines, TV, the Internet—all of them tell us the same thing: They have just what we need to make us happy, better, more attractive, more fulfilled versions of ourselves. And we buy it.

Do you have bad skin? Isn't that embarrassing? You need our product to clear it up. Or cover it up. Without that status car how can you walk with your head up? Here's the car that'll make you popular and earn you the respect you deserve. Are you in physical pain or discomfort? Your nearby pharmacy has a drug to make any part of you feel better. Emotional problems? Literally millions of Americans are taking drugs to even their feelings out.

None of these are necessarily bad. It's okay to want to look good, to have a decent car, to be healthy both emotionally and physically. In fact, it's better than okay. But culture moves us from a reasonable approach (taking care of yourself and finding balance in your life) to an obsessive approach (allowing these values to dictate your decisions and your way of life). How many people do you know who are totally obsessed with what's in their garage or closet or medicine cabinet or bank account?

[Ryan] *I recently took my Expedition in for a repair. First, let me tell you that this Expedition is my dream vehicle. I love it. It has everything I want in a vehicle, and I've added all kinds of upgrades. (Okay, after writing that last part I want to go back and delete it because I'm embarrassed by my materialism. But as Toben and I have said, we're still in process.) I picked up my truck, and as I was leaving, a salesman stopped me in the parking lot and asked about my truck.*

We chatted for a bit and then he asked what my monthly payment on my "old" Expedition was. When I told him, he said he could put me in a brand-new Expedition for less than I was paying now! My gut was screaming "Scam! Scam!" So I politely declined and drove away. But his offer stuck in my head. I could have a new truck! How cool would that be? Then it hit me: He could lower my monthly payment, but it would more than double my total car debt. And yet, even knowing this, I was still tempted.

Now, don't get us wrong. We realize that people don't pursue these delusions and obsessions *expecting* to crash and burn. Couples don't start a relationship, and then a marriage, planning for divorce. No one pulls out the credit card for the first or second or hundredth time intending to file for bankruptcy. And abortion is usually a desperate act by someone who feels she has no other choice. Our intentions are usually good. But even if we start out with good intentions, following culture's advice will always land us squarely in the middle of a really bad place.

Behind our actions—even some pretty stupid ones— often lies a good motive, even if it isn't obvious on the surface. For example, someone who's codependent is motivated by a desire to feel loved. That's certainly positive and reasonable, but if it plays out according to a worldly formula as codependence, it becomes destructive. Or look at the workaholic. He often just wants financial security or to contribute to others' well-being. Both of those are good things, but pursuing them on any path other than God's is harmful.

Culture works to corrupt positive goals and healthy desires so that we pursue them in destructive ways. Our purpose in aligning ourselves with Christ and standing against culture is to take a long look at our good motives and intentions and then figure out how to act on them in a way that's acceptable to God and beneficial to us and those around us. We need to discover the *whys* behind our actions, acknowledge the motives that are valid, and then act spiritually and responsibly.

So we're not trying to come down on anyone who has followed a normal motive to a harmful end. You feel bad enough without that. We're trying to expose culture for the lie machine that it is. The world teaches us to keep taking its medicine to get rid of the consequences of taking its medicine in the first place. But the consequences of listening to the world are unavoidable. And so is wreckage from bad decisions.

God's Blessing and the Good Life

Sorting out truth from fiction can be complicated. It's easy to confuse the pursuit and obtainment of culture's version of the good life with the pursuit and obtainment of God's blessing. But Jesus didn't die so that we could have the American dream; He died for something much bigger than that. And throughout the Gospels, He promised quite the opposite: that following Him would mean suffering and persecution in this lifetime. But let's face it: It's easy to get things tangled up. When circumstances are going well, we tend to believe we have God's blessing. When life takes a turn south, we feel God's absence or—depending on your theology—God's judgment.

Look back to a time in your life when everything was going your way. Your relationships, your job, your income, your housing situation . . . everything was good. Didn't you feel a sense of blessing? And the truth is that you may very well have been experiencing God's blessing.

Now flip it around. Remember a time when things seemed *not* to be going well. Maybe a relationship or two were out of order. Maybe you were having trouble finding a new place to live. Or you were having trouble making ends meet. Or you lost someone important to you. Did you feel like God was right there with you in that struggle, or did you feel like He was absent?

Our emotional state and our perceptions don't determine reality. We can *feel* blessed by a good thing that we've gained by sin. And we can *feel* abandoned or cursed when we've done nothing but obey God.

A whole segment of the church—the name-it-and-claim-it crowd—believes God wants us to have material success. They actually believe that the stuff we have is a testimony to God's work in our lives.

But ultimately the pursuit of stuff leaves us hollow.

[Toben] *Recently I had a change of perspective that revolution-ized my life and my family. I felt I had it all. I'm not bragging, but the fact is that we were incredibly blessed (as I defined it at the time). Great job, beautiful house, nice cars, two vacations a year, and all the other trimmings of the American dream. And for a while it felt like success, both in the eyes of the culture and in the eyes of the church. I felt like I had received God's full blessing.*

But something began to change internally. I looked at my life and realized that even though I always said my priorities were God, my family, and then my career, what I was living out was actually the opposite. If you added up the hours in a day and allocated them to each category, you got a totally different picture. My first priority was clearly my job.

I'd get up, get dressed, and leave for work before my girls were out of bed. After work, I'd spend a little time with the kids before they went to bed. After that I didn't have much energy to be the husband I had hoped to be. One day I realized that I was spending about two hours a day parenting (at best) and another couple of hours being a husband (at best).

Now, for a time I justified this by telling myself that my pri-mary responsibility to my family was to provide for them—to give them the stuff I thought they needed for happiness. My wife, Joanne, got a new car every couple of years, as well as extravagant birthday and Christmas presents. My kids went to a great private school, and they received everything they needed and most of what they wanted. For a while, everyone seemed happy enough.

If you had asked me at the time, I would have told you that my family was truly blessed. And I would have based that assessment on the material success I had achieved for my family. We were able to give a little money to the church and contribute to the building fund at the girls' school from time to time. God was on our side!

But I came to the realization that all this stuff wasn't leading me to become a better, more Christ-honoring person. In fact, I think that period was the lowest point spiritually in my whole life. I fell back into addictions during this time. I began to wrestle with depression (some of which I attributed to a spiritual battle for my soul), and I became increasingly distant from Joanne and the girls. I was a poor excuse for a husband and a father. I was physically present but relationally absent. We had it all financially, but emotionally and spiritually I was bankrupt.

This went on for more than a year, and it began taking a serious toll on my family. My attempts to buy my way out of face time and emotional availability weren't working anymore. The kids craved my time and attention, and their quality school and all-Nordstrom wardrobes couldn't take the place of my physical presence.

Sometimes I got frustrated and thought my family didn't appreciate my hard work for them. Sometimes I resented Joanne's demands on my time—time she wanted me to spend with her and with the kids. Suddenly the feeling of being blessed started to fade, even though we still had the material wealth I'd always equated with blessing.

33

*One day, as I was sitting in the notorious California traf-
fic—always a setting with plenty of time for reflection—something dawned on me. I'd even call it an epiphany. I was
miserable; we were miserable. My family wasn't connected
the way God intended us to be, and we certainly didn't have
the joy that's supposed to accompany true blessing. And it
was my fault.*

I saw that God's true blessing on earth was my family. Period.

*My thinking shifted, and my priorities followed. First off, I
started working from home three days a week. I was surprised
to discover that 20 percent of all employees in the United
States do this. I took Audrey and Emma to lunch once a week
and started a date night with Joanne. I fired the gardener and
started mowing the lawn myself. These changes may seem
small, but in light of the absentee father and husband I'd
been, this was a big step in the right direction.*

*Work changed, too. My company was acquired by a much
larger company, and it quickly became apparent that my job
situation—and my income—were about to change.*

*So my whole idea of blessing was turned upside down.
What culture promotes as the American dream felt like a blessing for a time, but in the long run it soured. Now, since I've
come to my senses the things that truly matter have come to the
top: I'm sold out to my family and committed to being involved
in their lives every day. My spiritual life still isn't where I want
it to be, but I feel closer to God, more dependent on Him, and
more assured of His presence in my life than ever before.*

I was never more miserable, more addicted, more sinful

than when I was living the "blessed" life my culture promotes. Jesus didn't come to earth to teach me how to be a good consumer. He came to teach me how to love Him and love others. That's the simple measure of my success.

[Ryan] I've faced my own struggles with what constitutes God's blessing. The majority of my income comes from speaking engagements—which means a lot of time on the road, away from home. It's a struggle sometimes; there's no other way to put it. Part of me wants more money, more possessions, and I feel driven to be on the road more to earn that money. Yet when I'm traveling, I just want to be home with my family. I don't want Laura to call and tell me that Lincoln laughed out loud for the first time or rolled over for the first time . . . while I was away. (Sadly, I did miss both of these baby milestones.)

So I have to ask myself, Is it worth it to be here? Is the money I'm making worth it? And for me, the struggle goes beyond that. My job is also a ministry. So I have to strike a balance: How do I book enough events to take care of my family without going overboard on commitments that keep me away? And in the meantime, how do I remain faithful to the ministry the Lord has called me to? That's the tightrope I'm walking.

The Danger of Buying into Culture

Culture's misguided concept of happiness and success has been ingrained in us by the thousands of messages we receive every day, from the time we're born until the time we die! The cumulative effect is that we believe two things: First, we're entitled to all the superficial values that culture promotes. And second, there's no room in this model for being a wrecked person. Jesus followers don't escape unscathed. If we buy into cultural lies, we will eventually taste the bitter consequences—feelings of worthlessness, depression, abandonment by everyone who's important to us, the destruction of our bodies . . . not to mention the implications when our soul goes out of alignment with God.

[Toben] *If I'm honest, I can attribute most of the times that I've been inextricably wrecked to my own selfishness. My abuse of alcohol was no exception. My drinking stemmed from a sense of entitlement: Culture told me I deserved to do whatever I wanted, regardless of the price others might pay. And I bought it.*

I'd wake up most mornings telling myself, Today I'm not going to drink. I can't remember ever waking up thinking, I can't wait to get blasted today. But as the day went on, maybe something would go wrong or upset me, I'd feel stressed or tired, and usually around one o'clock I'd convince myself that I deserved a drink after work. Just to take the edge off. Soon I'd start really looking forward to it, and then I'd obsess about it until I couldn't wait to leave the office. My only thought was to sate my desire.

Now at the same time, somewhere in my brain I would play out the eventual scenario. I knew that if I gave in to my selfish-

ness, I'd be out of commission as a father and a husband that entire evening. But my selfishness, my sense of entitlement, overrode it all. I believed the lie that it was all about me. Eventually God helped me get outside myself, but it was a painful, difficult road getting there.

When we follow culture's advice to buy or medicate our way out of wreckage as quickly as possible, we miss out on the potential benefits of the pain. We're encouraged to move a thousand miles an hour, or to fill our lives with noise and activity to keep our minds distracted and occupied. But that leaves us no time or silence for introspection, and we fail to learn the lessons that are part and parcel of the wrecked life. Numbing ourselves to the pain doesn't help us heal or move on. It's only when we're willing to sit in the wreckage and deal with it head-on that we can make progress.

In the long run the world's path to success falls short of the happiness and wholeness we're really looking for. Have you heard of the "quarterlife crisis"? It usually occurs in people between the ages of twenty-one and twenty-eight, usually after college or shortly after a person enters the "real world" of work, relationships, and responsibilities. At the writing of this book, Wikipedia lists its characteristics as:

- feeling "not good enough" because one can't find a job that is at his/her academic/intellectual level

- frustration with relationships, the working world, and finding a suitable job or career
- confusion of identity
- insecurity regarding the near future
- insecurity regarding present accomplishments
- reevaluation of close interpersonal relationships
- disappointment with one's job
- nostalgia for university or college life
- tendency to hold stronger opinions
- boredom with social interactions
- stress rooted in financial issues
- loneliness
- desire to have children
- a sense that everyone is, somehow, doing better than you

People have all kinds of explanations for this condition, but perhaps at the core it has something to do with an unfulfilled promise—the promise that cultural values will somehow make us feel complete. We become disillusioned when the emotional and spiritual payoff doesn't arrive. In our dissatisfaction with our lives, that's when many of us chuck the church.

But as long as we are looking to anything besides God to fulfill what is lacking inside us, we will end up disappointed. Only God, our relationship with Him, and our relationships with others will count for anything and provide God's truest blessings.

So how do we change the way we live and walk in this cultural minefield? How do we take off culture's eyeglasses and view the world as clear-eyed Christ followers? This isn't a book with easy answers, but here are a few ideas that have helped us.

For starters, the beginning of healing and healthy living is honesty. It's so easy to fall into the trap of rationalizing our actions. Isn't it funny that we think we can justify our poor thinking and wacky behavior to God? But we can tell you from our own experiences that God sees right through our feeble attempts, so we might as well be honest—with ourselves and with Him.

We also need to live honestly with others in Christian community. When we open up our lives to other believers—when we spend time with them, eat meals with them, and share experiences with them—we have the opportunity to get input from each other about our faulty thinking. Now, this can be tricky. We've all been around believers who wield their opinions like a hammer, slamming everything that *they* feel is bad. So we need to be selective; we need to choose trustworthy, safe people. Once we've found those people, we need to do the hard things—invite their insight, be vulnerable, be real and authentic versions of ourselves before these friends. We need to give them permission to speak into our lives.

Another way we can rewire our thinking is by practicing a few disciplines. When we come to God regularly through Scripture and in prayer, we give Him the opportunity to speak into our lives. We need to intentionally give God permission to speak truth to us, just as we do with friends and family, opening up and asking Him to communicate with us.

Finally, we have to be careful about what we're taking in. There's no way to listen to degrading music or look at crud online that tears women down and turns them into objects without having it affect our own thinking and behavior toward them. It's impossible to look at page after page of perfect people in magazines without distorting our body image and self-perception.

Most of all, it's important to remember that this fight for right thinking isn't a one-shot deal. It's a constant battle we'll fight as long as we live in this world, bombarded by this culture.

The good news? We don't have to go it alone.

Oh Church,
Where Art Thou?

[Toben] *I attended a church in California that did an amazing job of dealing with hurt, wounded, and generally wrecked people. In fact, its entire ministry was built around the notion that outcast people need a place to worship God.*

You could tell just by walking into the place that they were serious about this vision. You've probably never seen such a ragtag group of believers (and unbelievers) gathered together in a church. We met in a warehouse, but it was no less a church than the most ornate places of worship I've seen. The majority of us there were young(ish). Lots of tattoos, lots of diversity, lots of ratty clothes—sometimes because it was cool and sometimes because ratty was the wearer's only option. I saw a lot of struggles in people's lives—relationship stuff, work stuff, bills, homelessness . . . life stuff. And the leaders of this church were serious about dealing with all of it.

The pastor would typically start a service by preaching the gospel—just laying it out there plain for everyone to look at. Often he would mix in a tough topic, like pornography or living together before marriage. And at the end of his sermon he would say something like, "Okay, so who is buried in credit card debt?" And believe it or not, people would raise their hands! He would ask them to come forward . . . and they did! People from the church would lay hands on these folks and pray with them. When appropriate, the church would provide practical support and guidance, such as a credit counselor as a resource for anyone who wanted help.

This scenario was repeated weekly. People would admit their sin, come forward, and receive prayer and help. I saw life-changing trust, respect, and openness in connection with all kinds of issues—sexual abuse, pornography, and addictions of all kinds.

Now, this is a real church with real people. And others like it exist throughout the world. But unfortunately they're far from the norm; they buck the trend. (You might notice that we decided not to mention this church's name; we didn't want you to get jealous!)

When it comes to dealing with wrecked people, we feel the church needs to be taken to task a bit. Understand that we love the church and believe it to be the bride of Christ, nearly and dearly loved by God. So whatever we say, take it in that context. And note that our negative generalizations don't apply to all churches; you may be fortunate enough to be part of a congregation that's doing the important things right.

Unfortunately, when it comes to knowing what to do with wrecked people, most churches are as out to lunch as the culture. We remember all too well what it was like to grow up in the church. There's a reason for the perception that the church is made up of two-faced people who spout religious words but live by a very unreligious set of standards. Not all churchgoers fit this image. But you know what they say about the few bad apples. . . . Normal people with normal problems need only a few painful Sunday-morning encounters to feel burned by the very people they should trust most. If you have a personal history with church, see if the following scenario doesn't resonate with you.

We would get up early on Sunday morning, put on nice clothes, and head out the door to church. Sounds simple enough. But Sunday mornings always managed to be self-sabotaging; something always kept things from running smoothly. Almost without fail, by the time we piled into the car, someone was upset or stressed. A lot of the time it had to do with not wanting to go to church in the first place, but we were from Christian families. We do church. Like it or not.

So there we were in the car, wearing nicer-than-everyday clothes, practicing our plastic smiles to cover up the tension.

43

Wishing we were still in bed.

We got to church and filed into the pews. And regardless of our true inner state, we went through the motions—stand up, sit down, stand up, shake hands, sing three songs, sit down, sermon, one more song, and out the door.

Rinse and repeat . . .

Maybe you didn't grow up in the church, and this whole experience sounds a little foreign. You've probably formed opinions about the church and its authenticity in other ways. Maybe you have a relative who never misses a worship service but cheats on taxes. Maybe you had a religious parent who was all smiles in church but just plain mean at home. Maybe you heard on the news about a religious leader who talked one way and lived another.

This wasn't what God had in mind when He thought up the church. His idea was a lot closer to the picture we see in Acts 2:42-47:

> They devoted themselves to the apostles' teaching and to the fellowship, to the breaking of bread and to prayer. Everyone was filled with awe, and many wonders and miraculous signs were done by the apostles. All the believers were together and had everything in common. Selling their possessions and goods, they gave to anyone as he had need. Every day they continued to meet together in the temple courts. They broke bread in their homes and ate together with

glad and sincere hearts, praising God and enjoying the favor of all the people. And the Lord added to their number daily those who were being saved.

This group of believers did life together—they learned together, prayed together, ate together, shared their stuff . . . and someone new fell in love with Jesus and joined up every single day! Picture yourself there, in a Jerusalem synagogue or a home church, or worshiping at the Temple. Always with friends. Living among authentic people. True community. Can you imagine it?

So what happened between Acts 2 and now? Why is today's church picture so different? Well, first we have to remember that the church is made up of people, and people are deeply flawed. Anytime you're dealing with humans, you know things are going to go wrong.

Also remember that we're all hungry for acceptance and approval. When we go to church, the easiest way to get pats on the back seems to be . . . perfection (or at least faking it convincingly). This isn't a new idea. Look at the Pharisees—they were all about looking good and calling attention to themselves. Everyone thought these guys had it made, but their Oscar-worthy performances were covering up some of the deepest personal insecurities known to humankind.

Now, just because we can understand some of the human whys behind the church's failure, this doesn't let the church off the hook. God still expects us—individually and corporately—to deal openly and genuinely with brokenness. Jesus challenged the religious leaders of His day to drop their hypocritical masks, and He expects no less of us.

Unfortunately, we see "sin behaviors" running just as rampant *in* the church as *outside* the church. Christians do all kinds of terrible, dumb stuff, and the church can't afford to be silent about it. If anything, we should talk *more* openly about our problems than the world does. Then we wouldn't come off looking so hypocritical. Brennan Manning says that one of the main reasons for disbelief in the United States is that the things we Christians profess with our mouths, we don't live out in our everyday lives (our paraphrase). Churches are full of wrecked people who need help. You have these crowds of desperately wounded people, all standing around talking a good game. And usually that's exactly the way it stays.

In the Gospels, Jesus promoted some radical ideas about the church. He said that we're supposed to go to where the hurting people are. But most of the time we expect them to come to us. Jesus said:

> When the Pharisees saw this, they asked his disciples, "Why does your teacher eat with tax collectors and 'sinners'?" On hearing this, Jesus said, "It is not the healthy who need a doctor, but the sick. But go and learn what this means: 'I desire mercy, not

sacrifice.' For I have not come to call the righteous, but sinners." (Matthew 9:11-13)

Makes sense, right? Who most needs a doctor? The sick, not the healthy. But church people (and that includes us) don't often go out of their way to make house calls. Or, to use another medical analogy, it's like our church buildings and other meeting places are a doctor's waiting room. We all sit in the pews or on living room couches, glancing around, assuming everyone else must be a little sick. Otherwise they wouldn't be there. Of course, no one tells each other—fellow sickos—what's wrong with them. That's a conversation you only have with the doctor. So we sit and read year-old magazines, hoping the doctor will show up soon and heal us.

47

But the irony here is that we're not supposed to just stare at each other blankly in the waiting room. God has already recruited every Christ follower to get involved—to be part of His healing team. Fellow patients are *exactly* the people we should be telling about our problems. That's one of the ways God heals us.

[Ryan] *Church was a normal part of life for my family, until I hit fifth or sixth grade. Focus on the Family hadn't exploded yet, so I felt like any other kid in my class. But when Focus took off, everything changed. None of us knew what to expect. All of a sudden my mom and dad, who are (or were) fairly private people, were thrust into the spotlight along with my sister and me. Before the Big Change, we would leave church at a leisurely pace with everyone else, talking with friends. But after Dad's books and radio program became so well known, people would follow him out, clinging to him for advice. Other families went to eat; we'd wait an hour or more for Dad to finish.*

All of a sudden, I felt like we were living in a fishbowl. And none of us were allowed to be your average goldfish anymore. Christians now expected us to be special. And I wasn't. Over the years, I got countless questions—not really questions, more like criticisms or scoldings—that started something like, "Ryan Dobson"—hear the emphasis on the world-famous name?—"what do your parents think about . . . ?"

"What do your parents think about your skateboarding?"

"What do your parents think about your wearing a black T-shirt?"

"What do your parents think about your hair?" (when I had long bangs, à la Tony Hawk)

And again, "What do your parents think about your hair?" (when I went back to a flattop)

I was just being a kid. But I always wondered what I was doing wrong.

I still get those questions. In fact, one popped up at a music festival where I spoke this past weekend, and two in e-mails since then. For years I felt like I could never live up to my last name. Someone was always going to take me to task for some petty discrepancy in my life.

And if not me, then certainly my parents. I'm sure they

heard, "Did you know that Ryan [fill-in-the-blank]? What are
you going to do about this?"

Ironic. My parents were the ones who bought me the
board, the clothes, the haircuts!

I can see the absurdity of it now, but it was very frustrating
for a while. If you can't be yourself at church, where can you?

[Toben] In my family, things were complicated by the fact that
my sister was mentally ill and was gradually ripping our family
apart. She started to act out in kindergarten and on and off for
years until she was institutionalized. She would act up, freak
out, and wreak havoc on our family.

In the more public parts of a Sunday morning—the chatting
and hand shaking on the way in, the large worship service—
we looked like the most normal family. Those settings weren't
conducive to sharing sensitive family issues.

My parents were very involved at our church, and they
attended a big Sunday school class—a more informal setting
that seemed a good place to share vulnerably. So they did. Big
mistake.

When the senior pastor got wind of the struggles in our
home, he laid down two mandates: My mom should no longer
work, because apparently my sister's problems were exacer-
bated by my mom's working. (Mom worked from home and
was always around for my sister and me.) And my mom could
no longer teach Sunday school.

Imagine how this encounter rocked her! She had shared
something from her heart with a group of people she trusted

and ministered with, only to have that information thrown back at her, loaded with harsh criticism.

That wasn't the end of it. Over our years in that church, my parents were bombarded by criticism and advice from all directions:

"You aren't praying enough."

"You need to change her diet."

"Is there some sin in your life that God's dealing with through this situation?"

It went on and on. It was exhausting, and the cumulative effect was to make the church unsafe for us. My family and I realized that if we were going to survive church, we needed to keep the bad stuff—the hard stuff, the real stuff—to ourselves. The church was unable—or unwilling—to deal with our family's wreckedness.

Maybe this painful, alienating type of experience has been as real for you as it has been for us. Maybe you've suffered some form of church abuse because you told people "too much" of your life's reality, and it backfired on you.

[Ryan] *I recently heard a pastor say, "If you want to play games, there are a whole lot more fun games than church." I realized that I was playing this game too. When Laura's mom passed away, people would ask, "How are you doing?" and my automatic response was "Fine, thanks." But it would hit me that we weren't doing fine. We were totally at the end of* *our rope. We were barely coping with life and needed support. Why weren't we asking for it? Why did we give lame, superficial answers to people around us? Well, because it was easier to give in to the temptation to play the game and not truly live.*

I started wondering what kind of environment I was creating through my pseudo-communication. Was I creating an atmosphere where wrecked people around me would be comfortable sharing their struggles and pain? I didn't think so. I knew something had to change. If I wanted people to be open with me, then I had to be open with them, no matter the consequences.

Some people don't want to hear that you're not "fine." You'll see it in their faces or hear it in their responses. That's how you'll know who's playing games and whom you can count on.

Why the Church Comes Up Short

The church's inability to deal with wrecked people derives from a lot of complex causes. But two factors stand out: The church is made up of flawed people (like all of us). And even the church can't escape the seductive influence of culture.

The philosopher Immanuel Kant believed that everything we are today passes through the grid of our past experiences. In other words, in our churches, from the kindergarteners to the pastors, everything we think and do passes through a filter of personal history—the archive of our past experiences. We are unavoidably part of our culture, and the culture soaks into us subtly, without our awareness. Our perceptions and behaviors as part of the church are inevitably influenced.

Our cultural filters affect our reading and interpretation of the Bible, the way we think about what is good and godly and right . . . and our wanting to do it. None of us can escape culture, no matter how hard we try. It's like a rushing river that carries everything downstream with it. Even church leaders aren't exempt. They grew up and live in this world just like anyone—watching TV, reading books and magazines and newspapers, listening to the radio, looking at billboards, surfing the Internet. As they lead the church, culture's insidious reach is always part of the mix. Some fight it. Some go with it. Few really know how to beat it.

So we shouldn't be surprised if the church is no more an expert on being wrecked than the culture is. Of course, the church comes at it from a different angle. Instead of saying that *stuff* will get you out of your wrecked situations, the church points to *faith* (and all too often a watered-down version of faith) as the escape hatch.

Now let's be clear: Faith in Jesus Christ is literally the only way to receive salvation and to live well for God. For most of us it's the single most important part of our lives. But by "faith," the church often means an arsenal of "spiritual" behaviors. Most of these are actually valuable habits for a healthy Christ follower to develop, so we're not knocking them. But—and you may not like to hear this—no collection of spiritual habits, by themselves, can provide a cure-all. Not without other ingredients in God's healing recipe, like relationships, authentic sharing, unconditional acceptance, a safe environment, and sometimes professional help. And even with all of these, some kinds of wreckedness still don't go away.

Some people will tell you that if you lead a more godly life, you'll get out of whatever bad situation you're in. If you pray more, then things will start looking up. Maybe you need to have a quiet time every morning, or a *longer* quiet time. If you've spent any time in the church while you were wrecked, you've no doubt heard or received this kind of advice.

Just Say No

Think about people you know who are seriously struggling with some behavior that has them wrecked. If they're brave enough to come clean about their problem in the church, chances are the message they hear back is, "Stop." Yeah, right. As if it's that simple.

Sounds a lot like the big anti-drug effort in the eighties. Ronald Reagan had declared a war on drugs, and his wife, Nancy, was leading the "Just Say No" campaign, aimed at the children of America. The ultimate three-word answer was everywhere—on shirts and the evening news. Even the TV show *Diff'rent Strokes* had a guest appearance from the First Lady.

But is it really that easy? That little catchphrase doesn't

even come close to touching the reasons people take drugs. We're supposed to believe that, in a moment of crisis, three words are going to rescue me (or you) from a desperate craving?

We have a friend who struggled with homosexuality for much of his adult life. He kept it to himself for years, but finally in his small group Bible study with some safe male relationships, he came clean.

To complicate things dramatically, this guy was a husband and a father. He was an amazing, committed man, deeply involved in his church, who had harbored a painful secret for twenty years. And finally he found the courage to let it out. Everyone recognized that he didn't *want* to be gay; he was honestly struggling against his feelings. But when he came out, the guys in his small group, including the senior pastor, had no idea how to respond. Here was a guy they all loved. But this was totally uncharted territory.

So they did two things. First, the group suggested accountability; if this guy was considering doing something he knew was over the line, he was supposed to call one of the other guys for help and encouragement. (But no one wanted to get that call . . . or at least that was our friend's impression.) And second, some in the group basically told him to cut it out, to get over it and get back to being a good Christian man. (Others in the group were considerate enough not to say something so insensitive, but even the most understanding among them was stuck as to how to proceed.)

So what did our friend do? Well, the mixed and hesitant response to his confession kept him from feeling the freedom to tell how deep this issue truly ran. Everyone was obviously uncomfortable and at some level feared becoming tainted themselves. So instead of looking to the group for further support and encouragement, the man buried his struggles even deeper inside. And we all know that when a sin is buried and kept in the dark, it festers and becomes more toxic.

The man went deeper into the homosexual lifestyle, to the point that he felt he couldn't fight it anymore. He started visiting gay bars and getting into pornography, and he eventually ended up having an affair with another man. Then he *really* came out. Instead of confessing to homosexuality as a struggle, he announced it as his identity. And everything fell apart. The church was intimidated, clueless, paralyzed. Our friend decided it wasn't a good place for him anymore, so he quit the church. His small group friends experienced a range of emotions, but the main one was anger toward their sinning brother, which drove him further away. Most of those relationships were completely severed.

Let's break this down. First, make no mistake: This guy made some wrong choices and experienced the consequences of those choices. The church is in no way to blame for that. We also know that the problem wasn't lack of compassion or good intentions from the church.

55

Dozens of people were heartbroken by what had happened. The man was not shunned or asked to leave.

But the congregation felt powerless to do anything about it, powerless to help this friend and his family. He was obviously broken—completely wrecked by his choices—but the church didn't know what to do. (We're willing to bet many churches out there would be equally lost with a problem like this.)

The church failed him.

[Toben] *I can't say with authority what the church should have done in this situation. So let me speak for myself. I wish I had gotten in this guy's face and told him that no matter what he did, he wouldn't be able to shake me—that for better or worse I was his friend. No matter how he tried to leave, I was going to track him down and diligently pursue a relationship with him as a brother in Christ.*

I wish I had spoken the truth in love to this friend. I wish I had told him that I cared about him but that what he was doing was not cool. Somehow, without soft-selling, I would tell him the truth with compassion.

I wish I had worried a lot less about what other people thought. Jesus certainly didn't get stuck on that. He hung out with all kinds of people, many of them unsavory. Some of the self-righteous types took great pleasure in painting Jesus with the "sinner" brush because of the company He kept. But Jesus wouldn't let the paint stick. He defended His decision to love the outcasts, and He challenged His accusers.

Finally, I wish I had tried to find the story behind the story. Something was going on beneath the surface—maybe a spiritual battle or even past abuse. Who knows? But I should have taken the time to find out. If nothing else, maybe my compassion for him would have grown.

If I'd fought for this guy—if the church had fought for this guy—the story might have ended differently.

Maybe not . . . but maybe.

The Smell of the Church

The inability to deal with broken people is an indictment against the church. And against each of us.

Here's the irony: Everyone has a secret sin. Everyone has an issue that has real potential to wreck him or her. And if we don't think our church friends will understand and accept us with our sin, we keep it hidden. The sin grows in darkness, we dig ourselves in deeper, we fall a little farther away. Right under the noses of our oblivious brothers and sisters, who could help us.

In the process, a putrid atmosphere develops in the church—something you can almost smell. You walk in, and you detect something ugly, something everyone wants to keep buried deep inside.

We were in a church service once in which the pastor was attempting to talk about sin. He used an illustration from his own life . . . he ate too many sweets! Now if you're in the pews and you hear that and you're harboring a pornography addiction or you can't stop sleeping with your boyfriend or you're a drug addict, what's going through your mind? Either this guy is clueless about how to deal with *real* sin or he's too scared to expose his imperfections. Yeah, we know . . . sin is sin, no matter how big or small. But in church we seem to deem certain sins "approved for discussion" and others completely taboo.

Sadly, most churches have a tangible ambiance that says, "Keep your wrecked self tucked away. It's more than we can handle here." Yes, it's true that pain stemming from being wrecked in a bad way is often self-inflicted. And the church doesn't have a lot of tolerance for people who find themselves lying in beds they've made for themselves.

Now, if you're a victim, that's different. Then you don't have the guilt or sin stigma mixed in with your problems. But if you messed yourself up, God help you!

Are we saying that Christ followers should condone sin? No. Scripture is pretty clear about that. But it's also clear that, while we must utterly hate sin, we're also commanded to accept and love sinners. Sometimes we forget that second part. We lump the sin and the sinner together into one big hated bundle.

We pray from the pulpit, "God, be with those who are suffering, those who are in tough situations." But we do little to become part of God's answer to our prayer. Maybe your church has a grief recovery workshop or something for divorced people or maybe a twelve-step group or two. That's good. But a lot of bad stuff happens to all of us, and we need a way to deal with it in the everyday life of the church. In our experience, this is woefully lacking.

Being wrecked is often one of the very things that drive people to the church and to Jesus, so we need to be prepared to deal with that wreckage. We've heard countless testimonies of people who were entirely down and out and realized Jesus was their only hope. No doubt you've noticed that hard times are one of the biggest reasons people accept Christ. When life is all sunshine and blue skies, most of us don't see or feel the need for Him. But disaster has an amazing way of waking us up.

And yet, most believers are dozing off in the hospital waiting room.

What to Do!

Okay, so the church feels inexperienced and intimidated when wrecked lives walk through the doors. What do we do about it?

First, we each have to take personal responsibility to help change the church culture. That doesn't mean standing up in a service and yelling at everyone for sitting on the fence, apathetic and safe and distant. It means we start with ourselves and our individual responses to wrecked lives. Others' lives . . . and our own.

We need to open up about our own wreckage. If we keep our pain and problems to ourselves, so will others. Each of us can become a leader in a group, through our actions if not by our title: taking the risk first, setting the tone, and paving the way for others to share. We can open doors to freedom. This is the "going first" principle.

Think about the last time you were in a Bible study or other small group. When sharing about your lives, if the first person or two say nothing but "Life is fantastic" and "I'm so blessed" (even if they're faking it), others in the group aren't likely to bring in the dark thunderclouds of their miserable lives. They think something must be unacceptable about them if they can't be as happy as everyone else seems to be. It's simply part of group dynamics and human nature.

But if someone starts out with authenticity and openness, the rest of the group will likely follow suit. So go first!

60

[Toben] *I've spent some time in AA meetings for my drinking problem. One of the basic tenets of AA is acknowledging our need for a "higher power." (Those of us who are Christians acknowledge Jesus Christ as that power.) Most of the folks in these meetings have realized their need for someone to help pull them out of the mess they've made of their lives. And that point of realization usually turns out to be when they were at their very lowest. They often talk about a "moment of clarity" when they came to appreciate their need.*

You might be surprised how much the church can learn from an AA meeting, especially about how to deal with people's wreckage.

When I walk in, the first thing I notice is the smell. Actually, I pick it up half a block away. Cigarettes and black coffee, waft-

ing from small clusters of men and women smoking and drinking coffee from Styrofoam cups. To many of these people, that smell represents friendship and belonging. I say hi to a couple of familiar faces as I enter the small cinderblock room. I'm a regular, so most of the time I don't receive a special greeting. But someone is always there to welcome the newcomers.

The secretary (each meeting has one) sits at a table surrounded by a circle of about thirty chairs. She calls the meeting to order, and typically about twenty people take seats around the circle. We always start with a reading from the Alcoholics Anonymous Big Book.[2]

In essence, the reading reminds us who we are and where we've come from. It emphasizes our need for help in this ongoing battle against addiction: "Remember that we deal with alcohol—cunning, baffling, powerful! Without help it is too much for us. But there is One who has all power—that One is God. May you find Him now! Half measures availed us nothing. We stood at the turning point. We asked His protection and care with complete abandon."

Then someone reads the twelve steps, to remind us of the commitments we've made in our recovery program. We:

1. Admitted we were powerless over alcohol—that our lives had become unmanageable.
2. Came to believe that a Power greater than ourselves could restore us to sanity.
3. Made a decision to turn our will and our lives over to the care of God *as we understood Him.*

---

2 Alcoholics Anonymous (New York: Alcoholics Anonymous World Service, Inc., 1976), 58–60.

④ Made a searching and fearless moral inventory of ourselves.

⑤ Admitted to God, to ourselves, and to another human being the exact nature of our wrongs.

⑥ Were entirely ready to have God remove all these defects of character.

⑦ Humbly asked Him to remove our shortcomings.

⑧ Made a list of all persons we had harmed, and became willing to make amends to them all.

⑨ Made direct amends to such people wherever possible, except when to do so would injure them or others.

⑩ Continued to take personal inventory and when we were wrong promptly admitted it.

⑪ Sought through prayer and meditation to improve our conscious contact with God *as we understood Him,* praying only for knowledge of His will for us and the power to carry that out.

⑫ Having had a spiritual awakening as the result of these steps, we tried to carry this message to alcoholics, and to practice these principles in all our affairs.

We all recite the last line of the reading together: "We claim spiritual progress rather than spiritual perfection."

Then we start to share. "My name is Toben, and I'm an alcoholic." The rules for sharing are simple: Stick to who you were when you were drinking, what happened, and who you are now. Sharing is not a time to soapbox or gossip. It's a time to tell your story, and in so doing to give help and hope to other struggling people. Sharing is almost entirely voluntary and is usually limited to five minutes. So I keep it short.

In other people's stories I hear echoes of my own. And in mine, I suspect that they recognize parallels with theirs. Some have been sober for twenty-five years, while others may still be hung over from their last drink. But in all the stories two themes are constant: I'm given hope and strength, and I'm reminded that I'm not alone.

So what can the church learn from AA? Well, the first two steps offer a good start: Each of us, no matter how squeaky clean we want to appear, needs to admit our powerlessness and our need for Christ. We're all helpless in the face of some sin in our lives, so we might as well own up to it and then follow quickly by openly acknowledging our need for a Savior.

In our churches, we would also benefit from sharing our stories—not just victories but failures too. When we do this honestly, we give a gift of hope and strength to others in similar situations.

AA could also teach churches that there's no point in showing up if we're not going to be honest. Really, what would be the point of faking it in an AA meeting? We all know we're there because we're drunks in need of help. Is the church so different? Whether we're willing to face it or not, we're all there because we're sinners in need of Jesus. Our hidden sin is our worst and most deadly enemy. We find life only by confronting and destroying sin. There's no point faking it in church, either.

Admitting that we're all broken and in need of Jesus frees us to create a church environment that's safe for wrecked people. So as you have appropriate opportunities—total transparency isn't always appropriate—let people know about your wreckage. Don't go walking up to total strangers and spilling your guts. If you're not sure of the right timing or settings, get some coaching from someone who does. When you do share from your heart, you'll be surprised at people's responses. Typically, they'll tell their own stories of being wrecked and what God is doing (or not doing) in their lives.

If this can't happen in the church, where can it happen? If you don't start the ball rolling, who will?

[Ryan] *I was already on my way to California when I got the call that Laura's mom passed away. It's normally a seventeen-hour drive; I made it in fifteen. Along the way I got an unexpected taste of true community.*

After driving through the night, I stopped by my favorite tattoo shop where one of my best friends, Sid, is a tattoo artist. When I showed up, Sid said, "Dude, you look horrible." And I said, "I am." I sat there and cried for a while. I needed time to gain my composure before I went to see Laura; I wanted to be strong for her. The guys in the shop were there for me, listening to me and praying for me. And after about ten minutes,

Rob, another artist, said, "All right, it's time to go. It's time to man-up. You've got to do this."

The guys in the tattoo shop had it figured out: One of the keys to authentic community anywhere—in a church or a home or a coffeehouse or a tattoo shop—is the ability to look and listen. There's a story behind every story; what we hear and see at first usually isn't everything. Listening is a skill we learn by practice. And when people know you're really listening—that you care—they'll trust you when you ask questions. You've earned the right to ask questions that go a little deeper, questions that uncover their ugly, painful wreckage, so that God's community can go to work repairing them. You need to ease into listening slowly, carefully. Just as it's inappropriate to walk up to just anyone and dump all our personal baggage, it's also unhealthy and intrusive to throw open someone else's suitcase. It takes time to cultivate a trusting relational foundation first.

Prayer is one of our best resources for changing the church. This may sound simplistic, but we too easily skim over this powerful tool. In our experience, asking God to direct our words and questions in a given situation is the best way to ensure that our efforts lead to good results. God will direct you. He'll let you know when to share a wreck from your life and when to push a little deeper with a friend.

The church is made of people, and if we expect to

change it, we have to do it one person at a time. We do this through individual openness and authenticity, listening with our hearts as well as our ears.

We are the church. And we can change the church.

The Wrecked Life:
Disobedience

One evening David got up from his bed and walked around on the roof of the palace. From the roof he saw a woman bathing. The woman was very beautiful, and David sent someone to find out about her. The man said, "Isn't this Bathsheba, the daughter of Eliam and the wife of Uriah the Hittite?" Then David sent messengers to get her. She came to him, and he slept with her.
2 SAMUEL 11:2-4

It all started so innocently. King David was just minding his own business—maybe he was a little bored—when he looked out the palace window. And there was Bathsheba! David suddenly decided that his life wouldn't be complete unless he had sex with her. So he summoned her to the palace.

From the passage it seems that David felt he was within his rights as the king to sleep with another man's wife. Scripture doesn't tell us how Bathsheba felt about it, but she must have, at the very least, felt terribly used. In David's mind, it was probably a one-time indulgence that would remain quietly hidden in his unrecorded, soon-forgotten history. But the affair didn't end there, and David didn't get away clean. Events almost immediately snowballed out of control.

Bathsheba was pregnant! Damning evidence. Imagine David's panic. Imagine *Bathsheba's*. To make matters worse, Bathsheba's husband, Uriah, was out fighting a war with the Ammonites and hadn't slept with Bathsheba in some time. So in desperation David called him from the battle lines and gave him multiple opportunities to be with Bathsheba so everyone would think Uriah was the baby's father. But in an act of incredible loyalty to his country and fellow soldiers, Uriah wouldn't leave the palace gate.

If David was desperate before, now he was frantic. Not the best frame of mind for decision making. He decided to have Uriah killed. He sent orders back to his general to put Uriah on the front line, then pull back and leave Uriah out alone to be killed. Who did he assign as courier to deliver this death sentence to the general? The doomed man himself. Uriah. (How twisted is that?)

David's treachery succeeded. Uriah was dead, and David was free to marry Bathsheba. Which he did. Bathsheba eventually gave birth to their son. It looked like David had beat the system; he'd avoided wreckage despite his sins. But in reality the train had already plunged off the bridge; it just hadn't struck the ground below yet.

First contact came when Nathan the prophet showed up and informed David of a key witness to his crime . . . God. David would indeed face consequences for his actions. More specifically, God forewarned, "Out of your own household I am going to bring calamity upon you" (2 Samuel 12:11). That's when David knew he was in serious trouble.

God struck David's newborn son ill, and the baby died. David had pleaded with God for the life of his son, but when he recognized the finality of this consequence, he got up, cleaned up, comforted Bathsheba, and went on with life.

In a lot of ways, this represents the end of David's glory days. Later we see David betrayed by those close to him and fleeing for his life. His own son Absalom rebelled against him and plunged the entire kingdom into civil war. And the consequences of David's sin weren't limited to *his* life. Nathan told David, "By doing this you have made the enemies of the Lord show utter contempt" (2 Samuel 12:14). That's the way sin works. It sends out ripples—or tsunamis—that can have life-wrecking influence.

This tragedy reads like a textbook example of life on the wide path—the path of disobedience—featuring lust, power, sex, deceit, scheming, and murder. Now if David had been a bad guy, we might expect this kind of behavior, and we'd scoff when disaster struck. But David was a lot like many of us, and the sobering lessons from his life hit uncomfortably close to home. From childhood—long before he reached celebrity status—he was a faithful follower of God, just like so many churchgoers and believers today. In fact, the Bible calls David a man after God's heart (see 1 Samuel 13:14).

So how does someone like this—like *us*—end up so wrecked?

Triggers

David himself was frustrated and perplexed by his sin. Some of his reflections throughout the Psalms resonate with Paul's words in Romans 7:15-20:

> I do not understand what I do. For what I want to do I do not do, but what I hate I do. And if I do what I do not want to do, I agree that the law is good. As it is, it is no longer I myself who do it, but it is sin living in me. I know that nothing good lives in me, that is, in my sinful nature. For I have the desire to do what is good, but I cannot carry it out. For what I do is not the good I want to do; no, the evil I do not want to do—this I keep on doing. Now if I do what I do not want to do, it is no longer I who do it, but it is sin living in me that does it.

How often does this paradoxical drama play itself out in our lives? We're faithfully walking down the narrow path, and something catches our eye. Or our ear. Or our vivid imagination. It may be some small, momentary distraction. But we latch onto it and end up turned around and headed down the wrong path.

We might blow it spectacularly. Or maybe a string of little occasional indulgences gradually changes our hearts and adds up to big consequences. Or maybe it's a combination of the two, like it was for David. One unexpected eye-catching temptation—among many he must have encountered routinely—one significant moment of weakness, and suddenly he's guilty of adultery and murder!

Pay attention to this critical lesson. For most of us, our sins don't typically involve a great deal of planning. Sometimes they do, but more often than not we stumble into sin. We're ambushed by a trigger moment. David's trigger was a glimpse of a naked woman. (Why she was doing the rub-a-dub on her roof we'll never know.) And before he knew it, he was deep into something he never intended.

David had his triggers. So do we.

[Ryan] *God used a near-fatal experience as an object lesson about triggers in my life. One morning when I was still living in California, before I met Laura, I went to the beach to surf. There was a really big current heading south, and huge walls of waves were coming in. I put on my wet suit and started to paddle out. I paddled as hard as I possibly could for nearly an hour, but waves kept washing me back toward shore. I was becoming exhausted and frustrated, so I finally got out of the* *water. My body was so tired that I was seeing spots, and every logical part of my being was saying, "Just go back to your truck and call it a day. The waves are too big; they're just pushing you around." But as I walked toward my truck, I just got mad. I'd never been out this long and not caught at least one wave.*

So I went back and jumped in again. I was determined with everything in me to succeed. For another hour and a half I paddled relentlessly, constantly pounded by wave after wave. One time I fell off my board and almost didn't make it back on. I had to grab my leash and pull my board to me. I was grasping feebly to my board when reality dawned on me.

I was about to drown.

I was by myself—nobody in sight—and I had no strength left. Through my oxygen-deprived stupor I realized that if I got pushed off my board again, I might not get back on.

Somehow I managed to turn my board, point it toward shore, and grip with all my might. From there I let the waves push me back to the beach. They were going over my head—I was swallowing salt water and choking—but finally I made it to where my feet could touch. I couldn't walk. Mercifully a wave pushed me up on shore. I crawled a few feet before I collapsed. I finally got up the strength to walk back to my truck.

That night, lying in bed, I still felt like rubber. I remember the Lord impressing on me, "Are you really that dumb?" I knew He wasn't just talking about surfing. For quite some time I'd been allowing myself to be in situations with women where I could easily have failed morally—particularly with the woman I was dating. I was proud that I wasn't jumping into sexual sin, but we were repeatedly setting up tempting situations for ourselves, with no accountability in place. I kept telling myself that I was strong enough to resist temptation, that I was immune to sexual failure. I was persistently paddling out into waters that were way over my head. I was out there by myself, and the waves of sinful opportunity were pounding away at me, gradually sapping my strength. I was tempting death again and again; my strength would only hold out so long, and who could tell which "little" situation would take me past my limit? Which one would be the trigger, leading to disaster? I felt the Lord saying, "Ryan, you know you're in danger, and yet you keep walking into it. You've gotten away with it so far. Get out now, or you'll face some big consequences."

He'd been talking to me for a long time. Why hadn't I been listening? Why did I have to nearly lose my physical life to come to grips with my spiritual weakness against temptation? That day was a turning point. Later, when I became interested in Laura, I made sure I had accountability around me—I put safeguards in place. People asked me, "Is it because you're so weak?" And I'd say, "Yes—all of us are weak." We all know what triggers can trip us up. We need to be smart and find people we can turn to for help.

Triggers are usually private things, vulnerabilities that we, better than anyone else, know can pull us down. Your trigger might be a friend who gets you into trouble. Or the indiscriminate consumption of pornographic imagery that sets your mind racing and lowers your inhibitions.

The key to moral and spiritual survival is knowing what your trigger is and avoiding it like the proverbial plague, even if other people don't understand.

[Ryan] *I get many e-mails from guys and girls who've been checking their MySpace page or visiting some other innocent site, when out of curiosity they click on a link and suddenly they're viewing porn. Of course, that page has links to other pages that lead to even more mind poison, which eventually all adds up to an addiction.*

For some people, pornography is visual crack. And it happens so fast. One minute you're reading a message from a friend and the next you're looking at hardcore porn, and you have no idea how you got there. Well, if you're honest (and the e-mails I get are very honest), you can remember.

Lots of times, it just took one click. You knew what you were doing too. You could tell from the picture on the link that you should avoid it. But curiosity got the best of you, you moved the little arrow on the screen, and you depressed your index finger. Click. Some people can stop there, but for many others it's the start of a lifelong addiction.

Let me introduce you to Integrity Online (integrityonline. com), a service devoted to helping people guard against pornography. It offers software you can install on your computer that logs and e-mails any questionable Web sites you've visited to two accountability partners of your choosing. That way you'll think twice before clicking on that spam message. When recommending the software to people, I always tell them to choose their mom as one of their accountability partners. You're never going to want to look at porn with your mom.

Hello, My Name Is Toben . . .

[Toben] And I am an alcoholic. I wish I could say that I was a drunk before I came to Christ, but like David I fell after choosing to follow God. I had been a problem drinker for years after college but quit for about six years. Until January 2004, when I talked my wife, Joanne, into letting me drink again. See, I had a deal with her that I wouldn't drink, because in the past my drinking had caused her a great deal of pain. I started bugging her about it, and eventually she caved and said I could try drinking like a normal person. But if I couldn't control it, I'd have to stop again.

I remember that first drink like it was today's happy hour: a perfect martini . . . gin, very little vermouth, and three olives. From there I graduated to a couple of beers at home, then added a few more beers, and then accelerated to a case of beer. Two weeks was plenty of time to prove beyond doubt that I couldn't, in fact, drink like a normal person. I told Joanne I would quit. But I didn't; I just started to hide it.

I started doing a very dumb thing. Every day on the way home from work I would stop by a liquor store close to my house and buy two or three tall boys (sixteen-ounce beers, usually of fairly high alcohol content). Then I'd pound those down on the drive home. I timed it so that about the time the alcohol would hit my system I'd be parked in the driveway.

That's forty-eight ounces of high-octane beer consumed in about five minutes.

Then I would sneak out to the garage a few times each night to drink vodka. Bottom line: I was drunk from the moment I got home to when I went to bed—which was very early most nights because I was so hammered.

I know that alcoholism is a disease, but I honestly believe I chose my disease. I was no helpless victim. I knew before I took that first drink that if I could talk Joanne into it, I could start getting drunk again. And I liked that thought a lot. That first drink was a well-informed choice. So was my continued drinking after I said I'd quit. I made a choice every time I stopped at the liquor store or sneaked out to the garage. I know these were choices because I know what went on in my head. I would think, I don't need to do this. I should stop. *But then I would justify it and do it anyway.*

Implicit in these choices was another unintentional choice. For eight months I took a liquid vacation from my family. I was not a husband. I was not a father. I was simply gone. Only after I stopped did I become aware of the incredible damage I had inflicted.

And finally I made a choice to stop. I wish I could say that I had a moment of clarity one day while staring out over the ocean, or something profound like that. The truth is that I stopped because people who loved me intervened. I wish you could hear the passion in my voice when I say: If you can avoid being the subject of an intervention, please do so. It's terrible.

I was drunk at mine. Friends and family gathered around

me and told me that I was about to lose everything: my family, my job, our house. After sitting and sort of listening for a while, I basically told everyone where to go and went to bed. That night I started making plans to be homeless. I thought about what I'd take with me, where I would sleep. . . .

By the time I sobered up in the morning, it didn't seem like such a good idea anymore. So I called my uncle, asked him to find me an AA chapter, and went to my first meeting.

I went there thinking this would get everyone off my back and let me keep doing what I wanted. But something happened. In that first meeting on Sunday morning, the 27th of August, I felt God's presence telling me that I was in the right place and that I needed help. That I needed Him.

I went to eighty-five meetings in ninety days. I got sober. I got a sponsor. I worked the steps.

As of this writing, I'm three years sober.

We fool ourselves about the wide path. It looks like so much fun. But be warned: If you walk the wide path for long (sometimes not so long), you will be wrecked.

And it will definitely *not* be fun.

The Path to Death

Say that phrase out loud: The path to death. Sounds menacing, doesn't it? Well, it's supposed to. We don't mean to get all fire-and-brimstone here, but the point has to be made. The wide path is deadly. Fatal. One-way trip to the morgue.

This is obvious all over in the Old Testament, where people who opposed God were simply taken out. It happened in the New Testament, too. The story of Ananias and Sapphira is a tricky one. Their sentence was carried out *after* Christ died on the cross for the forgiveness of sins and ushered in the new covenant. Nonetheless, here's the account in Acts 5:1-6:

> A man named Ananias, together with his wife Sapphira, also sold a piece of property. With his wife's full knowledge he kept back part of the money for himself, but brought the rest and put it at the apostles' feet.

> Then Peter said, "Ananias, how is it that Satan has so filled your heart that you have lied to the Holy Spirit and have kept for yourself some of the money you received for the land? Didn't it belong to you before it was sold? And after it was sold, wasn't the money at your disposal? What made you think of doing such a thing? You have not lied to men but to God."

> When Ananias heard this, he fell down and died. And great fear seized all who heard what had happened. Then the young men came forward, wrapped up his body, and carried him out and buried him.

Three hours later Ananias's wife, Sapphira, came in and the story repeated itself: She lied. She died.

Pretty intense, huh? We don't claim to be biblical scholars, and we don't have deep, penetrating insights into why exactly this happened, but a few things are clear. Ananias and Sapphira lied flat out, grieving the Holy Spirit. And they died. On the spot. And get this next part: "Great fear seized the whole church" (Acts 5:11). For some time after this all went down, everyone was probably very, *very* honest.

When we're wrecked because of disobedience, we deserve death. Romans 6:23 says it bluntly: "The wages of sin is death." That's where the wide path leads us. Death comes in a variety of degrees. Most of the time, our sins introduce some small degree of death into our hearts. (Those add up, by the way.) But sometimes, as in the case of Ananias and Sapphira, the death our sin earns us is all-the-way death. Game over.

Most of us probably don't know people who have physically died because of their sin. But we know someone—or maybe we *are* that someone—who has experienced some sort of a spiritual or emotional death as a result of sinful choices.

[Toben] *This was certainly true with me when I decided to start drinking. In the process, I died emotionally for about a year. I was completely unavailable for friends and family and had nothing to give to anyone. I felt a little more of myself slip away every time I took a drink.*

We've all flirted with this kind of death. Any time we give in to our sin behaviors, we die a little bit, disappear a little bit, and life becomes a little more like hell. At some point, if we keep going, the asphyxiation will be complete.

The wide path is always before us, in one form or another. Sometimes it's via an addiction. Sometimes it starts with our thought patterns.

[Ryan] *When my dad had his heart attack, I felt like my world was collapsing around me. The person I looked to every day for guidance and advice and love and protection was being ripped away from me. And as if that weren't bad enough, it felt like my faith was being ripped away as well. I couldn't believe God would let anything like this happen to a faithful person like my dad.*

I didn't want to sit still in the middle of that pain; I wanted to run as far as I could from it. In the face of the grief and confusion and frustration, I started questioning everything I'd believed as my dad lay in the hospital bed. I decided I was done with Christianity.

But Christ wasn't done with me. He wasn't going to let me stroll down the wide path unchecked. He put me in a theology class with a professor who understood this snotty, arrogant, angry kid. This professor had the grace and the compassion to tell me, "It's going to be all right. We can learn from this. You can learn from this." He didn't throw it in my face or demean me or embarrass me. He helped me work through some of my bitterness and pain. He helped me back onto the narrow path.

What the Wide Path Will Cost You

When we blow it and find ourselves, by our choice, half
a mile down the wide path, we might hope against hope
that we'll get away with it, that we'll escape the consequences, that we'll get away clean. We may even bargain
with God—"This is the last time, I swear!" Or we might
brace for the consequences. We know they're coming, so
we hunker down and wait for the storm to hit.

Neither of these responses feels good, because somewhere down deep, when we blow it, we *expect* bad things
to happen to us. And if we fantasize that somehow we're
exempt from the cause-effect cycle of life, we certainly
expect negative consequences for *other* people who go the
wrong way. Think about your friends. When they do dumb
stuff or make bad life decisions, don't you expect them
to get payback? Don't you expect them to be wrecked by
their choices on this path?

Our point? In one way or another, we all know that
disobedience against God is costly.

[Ryan] *I used to fight when I was younger. Actually, I used to
get beat up. I can remember the first time I got pounded really
badly, and the worst part of the memory is that it was my fault.
I was in elementary school, and a bully lived in our neighbor-
hood. The first time I saw him, I was with my friend Jon, and he
pointed out said bully and gave me a stern warning against
getting on his bad side.*

Why warn me, you ask? Harmless, gentle moi? Well, I've

always been quick with words. Put this together with my typi-
cal failure to think very far into the future, and you'd often see
me exercising my verbal gift without considering the dire con-
sequences.

I lived wisely and safely for a few months, but it was only a
matter of time before my mouth got me into trouble with the
bully. I don't remember what I said; I just remember knowing
I was close enough to the safety of my front door. Upon hear-
ing my oh-so-witty comment, the bully chased me. I made it
into my house with all of an inch to spare. Now, I should have
slammed the door and left it at that, but that day I had a death
wish. I went to our front window and continued to taunt him
until he threw his tuna sandwich at the window, vowing to
exact revenge.

The day the bully caught up to me, I never saw it coming.
Jon and I were riding our bikes down our street when I heard a
strange sound. I looked back to see the bully bearing down like
a hellfire missile. He grabbed me by the neck, threw me off my
bike and onto the ground, and beat me silly. He only stopped
because Jon was pleading for my life. I don't remember how
many times he hit me or the extent of the damage. I do remem-
ber thinking, Oh man, you've got to control that stupid mouth!

Some people say, "No one ever deserves to get beat up."
Maybe. But whether or not I deserved that beating, I know I
could have avoided it. Yet I had knowingly walked into it.

That wasn't the last time my mouth got me into trouble. I
could tell you about a couple of other beatings I should have
rain-checked. And I almost didn't graduate college because

of my big, dumb mouth. I hold to some strong opinions, and back in college I would debate anyone, anywhere. For some reason—arrogance, naiveté, stubbornness—I couldn't stop myself from debating professors in class. Somehow I felt it was my duty to publicly express my disapproval, to confront what I perceived as injustice and ineptitude.

During my senior year I was involved in a small group project. I personally believed—and still believe to this day—that the assigned activity was inappropriate. I might even be right. But the way I handled it almost cost me my diploma. Instead of meeting with my professor in private, I decided I would lead our group's oral presentation and use that forum to express my views.

I was packing my apartment to move out of town when I got the call. I had failed the class. I quickly contacted my professor and asked on what grounds he had failed me. He said I hadn't completed our final assignment. (True.) He knew I would disagree with his verdict and welcomed me to present my case before the university court.

At that moment the Lord spoke to me. He said I was only hurting myself and that I had publicly disgraced a valued professor who was doing his best to provide a Christian education. I was at fault.

I quietly apologized to my professor and asked if I could retake his class during summer school. He graciously agreed. Instead of taking a trip with my friends, I retook his class.

I'm embarrassed that it took me so long to learn this lesson: It wasn't about the what, but about the how. Whether I'm right or wrong is one issue. But the way I respond is always my responsibility. Walking the narrow path means being teachable, being willing to apologize. It means looking in the mirror and admitting we make mistakes and commit sins. It's acknowledging that we still have a ways to go toward God's goal of maturity in character.

Why does denial come so easily to us? We know what we should do, and we definitely know what we *want* to do. We willingly walk the wide path and somehow trick ourselves into thinking that things are going to work out just fine. But the truth is, there aren't exceptions to this reality: The wide path always leads to wreckage eventually. This was true for David, it was true for a college student with an attitude, and it has been true of the friends and family members we've observed on the wide path.

Genuine success and fulfillment in life come only when we acknowledge and accept this. As long as we believe in consequence-free sin, we'll stray from the narrow path God has laid out, and we'll always wake up wrecked. And surprised. The wide path *will* leave its mark. There's no way around it. We get scarred, beat up, worn down. And then, even when by God's grace we get back to the narrow path, we bring those scars with us.

But the leftover scars aren't all bad. Sometimes it's actually worse to "get away with it" than it is to get caught. *What?* you ask. *You have to be crazy. You think it would have been better if I'd done the time or paid the damages or suffered the humiliation? Those things are, well, bad.*

Sure, they *feel* bad. But when you've done wrong and you bring it out in the open and deal with it, something very good happens. Something constructive. Getting caught allows us the opportunity to make amends, ask for forgiveness, and begin the work of rebuilding trust. Even more important, it forces us to confront and change the underlying thinking and values that led to our destructive decisions in the first place. Many of us would keep on hurting ourselves and others, getting into wreck after wreck, if we never got caught.

Besides, we never *really* get away with anything anyway. Some may never be caught, but no one gets away unscathed.

For example, we have countless friends who wrestle daily with guilty consciences. One man recently explained that he was sexually active in high school, some fifteen years ago. He remembers every girl he slept with. Those memories still haunt him. He now knows how much damage he did to himself and to the girls. He's a Christian, and he believes that he has been forgiven, but he can't shake the shame. His time on the wide path won't let him go.

[Toben] *I can honestly say that getting caught drinking was one of the best things that ever happened to me. Would I have said that at the time? Absolutely not. It felt utterly humiliating. But it saved my life. Granted, the consequences were significant: I had to dig myself out of a deep hole with friends and family. It's a terrible feeling when someone tells you that you've lost their trust and you're going to have to earn it back over time. I hate the waiting, the time it takes to prove you've really changed. In fact, I would have done just about anything to bypass that painful process. But it was the only path to healing. It was part of my journey along the narrow path.*

And I'm glad I walked it. Looking back now, after thirty-some months of sobriety, I can say that I have earned back that trust. My relationships with the people who were most affected by my drinking are healed today. If I hadn't been caught, I wouldn't have stopped, and my secret would still be eating me alive. I would still have been destroying relationships, rather than thanking God that they're better than ever before.

Do I still feel shame? Yes, I do. But it isn't in the front of my brain anymore. It sneaks up on me occasionally. Sometimes when I'm experiencing a tender moment with one of my girls, I think to myself, How could you have come so close to losing all of this? *And I feel shame. But more than shame, I feel relief that I stopped before I went that far.*

We may or may not get caught. We might keep our sins hidden, or they might be exposed to the light. But either way, we always bear the marks of those behaviors. Guilt may slowly gnaw away at us; memories can inhabit our waking hours or lurk in the background and sneak up on us from time to time. So when we finally recognize the unavoidable burden sin leaves on our hearts, shouldn't that be enough to keep us from ever walking the wide path again? For some people, yes, it's enough. But even the painful leftovers from past disobedience don't keep some of us from returning to it.

A Road to Restoration

Still, the fact of sin's lingering pain doesn't have to leave us hopeless. We can be restored to blessing, fulfillment, and usefulness even after a journey along the wide path. This is true because our disobedience and wrecked lives don't change the way God sees us. He still loves us, just as He loved David, and He can still use us in spite of—or even because of—the scars we sport.

After David's son died, Scripture says, "David got up from the ground. After he had washed, put on lotions and changed his clothes, he went into the house of the LORD and worshiped. Then he went to his own house, and at his request they served him food, and he ate" (2 Samuel 12:20). He comforted Bathsheba. After some time she gave birth to another son. His name was Solomon, and he came to be one of the greatest kings of Israel. God in His grace restored David to a life characterized by new blessings and good things.

But if you think David was unaffected the rest of his life just because God forgave his mistakes, you're missing the rest of the story. The prophet Nathan prophesied, "From this time on, your family will live by the sword because you have despised me by taking Uriah's wife to be your own" (2 Samuel 12:10, NLT). This prophecy was tragically fulfilled throughout David's life: His son Amnon raped his daughter Tamar; his son Absalom killed Amnon; Absalom slept with David's concubines; Absalom led a revolt against his father and was later killed violently; and Solomon arranged the death of another son. Redemption doesn't simply evict our personal demons; the repercussions of our sin sometimes cause us grief for some time. But while the consequences don't just disappear, Scripture promises that God does erase our guilt for our transgressions when we repent. Isaiah 1:18 says:

> Though your sins are like scarlet, they shall be as white as snow; though they are red as crimson, they shall be like wool.

Some of us might wish for spiritual amnesia, but God is able to redeem all kinds of bad decisions in such a way that our painful memories can even become tools for good. We saw this truth when God began using the wide-path pain of one of our friends as a tool to help others.

Liz was a self-professed "wild child" in junior high and high school. She was into all kinds of trouble. She slept around and eventually became pregnant when she was sixteen. She was expelled from school, but God got a hold of her. She made her way stumblingly to a local Christian high school, knowing that she needed a change—she needed something to go right in her life. The school admitted her, and that was the beginning of an amazing turnaround.

Now Liz is able to share with local high school girls, both individually and in groups, about her experiences in an attempt to help them avoid her mistakes. This positive outcome has totally reframed her thinking about her history and her worth. Does she wish she could have avoided that painful path? Absolutely! But she appreciates the fact that, as a result of her experience, God has given her a ministry that touches and changes the lives of girls who find themselves in the same situation.

Romans 8:28 says that God can use anything for good. This is demonstrated most clearly when, in spite of the pain, He allows us to learn from our time on the wide path and then gives us opportunities to use those experiences to benefit others.

A Fuller Life

[Toben] *I know a man, now in his seventies, who started a decade-long heroin addiction in his late twenties. He was a pretty normal guy leading a double life. He had a job, a house, a family . . . and a secret.*

Eventually his using caught up with him and supplanted everything of value—everything that was his life. Heroin had him. In the words of another friend, the drugs that had served him for years knocked on his door and told him that it was time he served them.

He was about forty when he finally experienced a moment of clarity and realized he needed help. Homeless and utterly alone, he stumbled into an AA meeting. He has attended a meeting almost every day throughout the last thirty years.

If you met him, even if you didn't know he's been a junkie, you would know this guy has had a hard life. He has a Keith Richards–type quality about him, looking like he has been kicked around and worn down. He's rumpled and wrinkled, beyond what you would expect at his age. He's stick thin and hunched over, and his hair—what's left of it—sticks out in all directions. He dresses in jeans and T-shirts and cardigans.

He doesn't say much at his AA meetings, but when he does, no matter what else is happening, people go silent. Everyone knows that his few words are always incisive. People treat him as something of a sage, drawn to his economically worded statements of wisdom.

When it's time for new members to select a sponsor, he's almost always on the top of their lists. As a sponsor, he's a no-nonsense guy. He lets his "sponsees" know that it's his way or the highway. You'll work the steps—the way he tells you to work them—read the Alcoholics Anonymous Big Book, come to meetings, and greet newcomers. He's . . . gruff. But if you do what he says, you have a good chance of beating your addiction. And if you spend some time with him and are able to look past his gruffness, you begin to see in him a deep underlying compassion—even affection—for people who are walking a path that he trod for so long, with such disastrous results.

A happy ending would be a nice touch to his story—the return of his career, his family, his house. But none of that has happened. He lives alone in an apartment and talks to his adult children infrequently. In that respect he still bears the marks of the time he spent on the wide path years ago. (Sometimes even returning to the narrow path doesn't bring back what we've lost.) But he is at peace.

I'm not sure if he's a Christian, but he is a spiritual man. He refers to his higher power as God, but who knows if that has led to a saving belief in Jesus Christ. Nonetheless, no one can deny the reality of God's blessing on a man who is walking according to some of God's principles. Here's a guy who has been through it all, seen it all, and done it all, who has turned his back on the wide path and now spends each day trying to walk the narrow path, as he sees it. In the process he has helped dozens, if not hundreds, of suffering people to begin (and keep on) the path to recovery.

We have a lot to learn from a guy like this. Yes, the specifics of each of our stories will be different. The time we've spent on the wide path leaves different marks on each of us. The attractions that drew us to that path are likely unique. The lessons we've learned along the way are distinct. And the way we use what we've learned is up to each of us individually. But all of us—when we've been wrecked by our disobedience, when we've spent our time hanging out on the wide path—can be assured of hope for restoration to a fuller, more compassionate life if we let God work in our lives.

Wherever you are on your journey—whether you're squarely on the narrow path or running amok on the wide one, whether you're covered with scars or have only a few—our message is one of hope. God is all about doing the work of redemption in our lives. No matter when we've entered the wide path—before becoming a Christian or after—or how much time we've spent wrecked by disobedience, Jesus Christ can still make something good of us.

The Wrecked Life:
Circumstance

cir·cum·stance (sûrkəm-stans), n., the sum of determining factors beyond
willful control. Often used in the plural: a victim of circumstance.[3]

— — —

*God, how could you let my wife die? I'd rather die too than
go on without her.*

*Of all places for the tornado to hit, why here? Why my
house? We've lost everything.*

---

3 www.thefreedictionary.com

I trusted him on that business deal . . . and now I've lost a friend and all my savings.

I moved across the country for him—we were going to get married. Now he says it's over. What do I do now?

Unfortunate circumstances. Are they something as simple and impersonal as being in the wrong place at the wrong time? No, that's a little too easy. And that definition implies that the things that happen to us—particularly the life-wrecking events beyond our control—are the work of fate. This denies God's role in our lives. No, our circumstances are far more significant than accidents and chance events. An almighty God who wants to see us grow and change can actually orchestrate our circumstances . . . for better or, to our perception, for worse.

Let's be clear: We're *not* saying that all things that happen to us, good and bad, happen at the hands of God. We don't have the expertise or space to fully unpack this issue—a task that would require a theology degree and about a thousand pages. But we do feel like we can contribute something to this question: Why do bad things happen to good people? We don't believe God *makes* bad things happen, that He intentionally ruins our lives through circumstances we can't control. But at the same time nothing that happens to us is outside of God's will. Before anything happens to us, God knows about it.

Let's set aside for now the life events that result from

our choices—happenings that are partly or completely
within our control. In this chapter, we're dealing with life
events that just *happen*—apparently having nothing to
do with our choices. And in this category called circumstances, we're also including events in which we're victims
of other people's choices . . . when there's nothing we can
do to prevent them. In all of these difficult times, somehow God can be, and is, present with us. As He promised
in Romans 8:28, He will work out those circumstances
for good if we love Him and are called according to His
purpose.

This is a fine line to walk. A lot of people don't believe
in an all-powerful God because they can't accept that
someone who is all powerful wouldn't stop all the pain
in the world. We'd like to believe that only good things
come from God and that He has nothing to do with the
bad times. But Scripture says (as we'll see shortly) that
He's involved with us in all our experiences, both good
and bad. He knows in infinite detail what our challenges
will be and when they will come; we're talking about a
God who knows the number of hairs on your head (see
Matthew 10:30)! When we're wrecked by our circumstances, we might think that God is gone. Or impotent.
Or unaware. Or stupid. Or cruel. But our "undeserved"
wreckage doesn't imply these things.

We'll unpack our reasoning as we go, but for now
we just want to make one point clear: As often as we're
wrecked by our bad decisions, our sins, our wanderings

on the wide path, we're also wrecked by circumstances. And God is there with us in those times.

Maybe the best example of this in the Bible—maybe the best example in *history*—is the life of a man named Job.

Getting to Know Job

"In the land of Uz there lived a man whose name was Job. This man was blameless and upright; he feared God and shunned evil" (Job 1:1). Sounds good, right? We'd all be proud of an epitaph like that.

And besides being a moral guy, Job had it pretty good in other ways too. He had a big, close family he loved, prayed for, and took care of physically and spiritually. And he was wealthy, with large flocks of donkeys, oxen, sheep, and camels. Job was pretty satisfied with his life; he was content.

And then all hell broke loose. Literally.

Because he was righteous, Job became a target. Satan, eternally at war with God, came up with a sinister wager.

> "Does Job fear God for nothing?" Satan replied. "Have you not put a hedge around him and his household and everything he has? You have blessed the work of his hands, so that his flocks and herds are spread throughout the land. But stretch out your hand and strike everything he has, and he will surely curse you to your face."[4]

4 Job 1:9-11

God accepted the challenge. He told Satan he could do whatever he wanted to Job, as long as he didn't lay a finger on Job himself. So Satan went to work.

> One day when Job's sons and daughters were feasting and drinking wine at the oldest brother's house, a messenger came to Job and said, "The oxen were plowing and the donkeys were grazing nearby, and the Sabeans attacked and carried them off. They put the servants to the sword, and I am the only one who has escaped to tell you!"
>
> While he was still speaking, another messenger came and said, "The fire of God fell from the sky and burned up the sheep and the servants, and I am the only one who has escaped to tell you!"
>
> While he was still speaking, another messenger came and said, "The Chaldeans formed three raiding parties and swept down on your camels and carried them off. They put the servants to the sword, and I am the only one who has escaped to tell you!"[5]

All in all, it was a pretty rough day for Job. Back then, people relied almost completely on their herds and crops for their financial security. Losing all those animals, along with the servants who ran the operation, would have been devastating. To put it in perspective, the modern

---

5 Job 1:13-17

equivalent would be a godly, wealthy person having all of his bank accounts and retirement funds entirely wiped out—in the span of a day. And circumstances were about to get worse. . . .

> While he was still speaking, yet another messenger came and said, "Your sons and daughters were feasting and drinking wine at the oldest brother's house, when suddenly a mighty wind swept in from the desert and struck the four corners of the house. It collapsed on them and they are dead, and I am the only one who has escaped to tell you!"[6]

Just when it seemed nothing else could go wrong, Job was dealt this crushing blow—news that no parent could ever be ready for. We might expect Job to react with rage, despair, resignation, bitterness. But his actual response catches us completely off guard.

> At this, Job got up and tore his robe and shaved his head. Then he fell to the ground in worship and said: "Naked I came from my mother's womb, and naked I will depart. The LORD gave and the LORD has taken away; may the name of the LORD be praised." In all this, Job did not sin by charging God with wrongdoing.[7]

6 Job 1:18-19
7 Job 1:20-22

Wow! Job unexpectedly, unwillingly swapped a best-blessed life (by any standard) for complete ruin. In the space of a chapter! Everything he had, everything he cherished, was destroyed. His wealth, his servants. And his children.

Put yourself in Job's sandals for just a minute. Feel your heart race and the adrenaline rise as one messenger after another runs up and reports absolute disaster. Feel, if you can, the shock and paralyzing grief, crushing down on you, smashing your heart to pulp.

Before all of this, if you'd asked Job what was the worst experience he could imagine, he probably would have said the loss of his wife or a child. How could he possibly have conceived of destruction beyond his darkest nightmares?

But get this: Job, in all his pain, didn't sin against God. "The LORD gave and the LORD has taken away." Don't get the wrong impression that Job was somehow blasé about his losses. He tore at his clothes and shaved his head in deep mourning. In one day he was hurt more than most of us are hurt in a lifetime. But this didn't keep him from being wise at the same time. He'd figured out long ago that everything came, undeserved by us, from the hand of God. He'd made a habit of holding on to the things of this world loosely. He felt desperate pain, but he stopped short of blaming God.

And Satan was ticked. So the devil appeared again in front of God.

"Skin for skin!" Satan replied. "A man will give all he has for his own life. But stretch out your hand and strike his flesh and bones, and he will surely curse you to your face."

The LORD said to Satan, "Very well, then, he is in your hands; but you must spare his life."

So Satan went out from the presence of the LORD and afflicted Job with painful sores from the soles of his feet to the top of his head. Then Job took a piece of broken pottery and scraped himself with it as he sat among the ashes.

His wife said to him, "Are you still holding on to your integrity? Curse God and die!"

He replied, "You are talking like a foolish woman. Shall we accept good from God, and not trouble?"

In all this, Job did not sin in what he said.[8]

Um . . . when your wife tells you to curse God and die, you know things are bad. Here this guy's just minding his own business, being as faithful to God as possible, and the next thing he knows, his family is wiped out, his wealth disappears, and he's covered with sores. Of all times, that's the moment his wife picks to tell him to just cash it in.

8 Job 2:4-10

Neither of us has ever been where Job was, so we can't imagine the devastation his wife's words must have piled on top of everything else that was going on. She was the one family member on earth he had left, and now even she had given up.

Now if you miss this one important fact, you miss everything: *Job didn't know why he was suffering.* In chapter 6 we'll talk about people who *know* they're suffering because of their obedience. But Job didn't have a clue why he had to go through all this grief. No explanation. No assurance of some clear meaning or purpose. Just unrelenting, incomprehensible pain.

Which helps us understand why, throughout most of his book's forty-two chapters, Job kept asking the question "Why?"

Why?!

Had Job known why he was suffering, his perspective would likely have been a little different.

[Toben] *Years ago I suffered a stomach problem, inconveniently timed to strike during a business trip. The pain started on the way to the LA airport and got worse and worse. I spent the flight doubled up in pain. When I got to Denver (on the way to Colorado Springs), the last leg of my flight had been canceled. So I had to ride the bus through a snowstorm down to the Springs.*

When Joanne picked me up, I said through gritted teeth,

"I have to go to the emergency room . . . now!" Unfortunately for Joanne, she was already in her pajamas. But by now I was literally moaning and crying and generally freaking Joanne out. So it was come-as-you-are at the emergency room.

I spent the next month in the hospital. I underwent two major surgeries and countless other treatments. When I first checked in, the surgeon said that if I hadn't come in, I likely would have lived only a few hours. Fortunately I had a group of doctors and surgeons who knew what they were doing. They saved my life.

A couple of points that resonate with Job's story: When I was on the plane and on the bus, not knowing what was wrong, I was terrified. The extreme pain couldn't be a good sign, but what was causing it? I was clueless. My pain was intensified by the fact that I was miles from home with no hope of help for hours. I felt some emotional relief once I reached the hospital; help was on the way. And even before I received any physical relief, I was set even more at ease when the doctors found out what was actually wrong with me. Knowing the reason for my pain, and having a plan to deal with it, took a huge weight off my mind, even though the physical pain hadn't yet lessened. We humans suffer even more greatly when we see no purpose or end to our agony.

Job wasn't afforded the luxury of knowing the purpose for his pain. Furthermore, he didn't know what, if anything, was going to make it better. For all he knew, he might have seen the last of his losses, or the grief might only have been beginning! That not knowing may have been as bad as the actual losses themselves.

[Toben] *One absolutely essential ingredient for my emotional survival during my hospital stay was my wife's support. Joanne was by my bedside constantly, leaving only to eat or shower when someone else took her place. She slept in a chair almost every night for a month. She took care of me and constantly offered words of affection and encouragement. She didn't have any answers to our whys either, but she stayed faithful. I can't imagine how devastated I would have felt if Joanne had said, "You might as well curse God and die instead of suffer through this." I think I would have given up hope altogether.*

When tragedy strikes, we go through the same process Job did: Our first instinct is often to look inward to figure out if somehow *we* caused the problem. If we find no personal culpability, we then look outward—what or who caused the calamity? That's when we might start blaming God, especially if our pain seems undeserved. We question Him and call out for relief.

We want to believe there's a reason for our suffering and that the suffering will come to an end; the idea of purposeless pain is hard to accept. So is indefinite duration. Like Job, we naturally struggle to figure out what's going on. Knowing *anything* that sheds light on our circumstances or situation can help us accept our plight.

In August 2007, a group of miners in Utah were caught

103

in a cave-in. For weeks no one knew if they were alive or dead, although the likelihood of their survival diminished with time. The mining company and rescue teams did everything they could to find the trapped men, boring holes 1,500 feet down into the mine shaft, clearing rubble, and using every available technology.

The miners' families were obviously desperate for their rescue. But they also became desperate to simply know what had happened. Any kind of closure—even confirmation that all the victims were dead—would be better than living with uncertainty. Eventually all concerned agreed that the men could not have survived this long, and recovery of the bodies was declared to be too risky. And now, even though the miners are certainly dead, their families continue to wrestle with unresolved questions.

When we can't figure out the *why* or *how long* of our suffering, it can become absolutely maddening. But even those aspects of our wreckage can serve a good purpose in our personal growth.

Didn't See *That* Coming

As is the case for most of us, Job didn't foresee the tragedies that hit him. Everything was going along quite nicely when suddenly he was blindsided by a series of one-two punches. He had no way of fathoming in advance the depth of loss he was about to face.

For most of us, it's the circumstances that come out of nowhere that have the most devastating effect. With some warning, we can try to brace ourselves; we can prepare mentally and spiritually. But the shock of the unexpected takes its toll.

[Ryan] *During the writing of this book, my wife's mom passed away. It was completely unexpected and couldn't have happened in a worse way. Laura was five months pregnant with our first child and had flown home so her mom could throw her a baby shower. When the plane landed, Laura called her mom from the airport. Her mom was complaining of chest pains, and Laura suggested she go to the ER. But her mom's doctor had recently examined her heart and told her she'd live to be a hundred. She'd wait until Laura got to her place and then go to the hospital if necessary.*

Laura arrived to find her mom unconscious on the floor. After a moment of paralyzed shock, Laura frantically called 911. In a daze, she started CPR. The paramedics arrived and took over, but it was too late.

Laura, a first-time mother-to-be, stood over the body of the woman with whom she'd been planning to celebrate her new baby's arrival. Instead, twenty-four hours later she was arranging her mother's funeral.

And the hits just kept coming. Days before that trip one of our puppies had gotten into a tube of Gorilla Glue. Now, you have to understand that Beanie and Burr may look like ordinary mutts, but they occupy a special spot in Laura's heart. We got Beanie the day after we moved to Colorado. She was an important companion for Laura, who'd left all her friends and family and the ocean she loved to come to a place where she knew no one. When Laura was upset, Beanie was upset; when Laura was pregnant and dealing with morning sickness, Beanie would come in and whine and rest her head on Laura's lap.

X-rays revealed that Beanie had a lump of glue the size of both my fists hardening in her stomach. So Laura was facing her mom's sudden death and a life-and-death emergency with Beanie. From one perspective, it might look like God was displeased with us and had sent these circumstances to punish us. But we believe otherwise; we know the character of God.

We wouldn't have voluntarily signed up for these circumstances, but now I can tell you that innumerable blessings were showered upon us as a result of that difficult season. Some of the situations got better (Beanie's surgery was successful), and others we just had to endure together, one day at a time. But in the midst of it, we were overwhelmed by the love and support of family and friends. My parents have an amazingly packed schedule, but they immediately bought tickets and flew to California to attend the funeral. My dad even spoke during the ceremony. I think weddings and funerals tend to bring out the best and the worst in people. This tragedy helped draw Laura's family together, and since then her dad has called her every day, even when he's out of the country.

As Laura and I drove the nineteen hours back to Colorado, we reminisced about memories of Linda. We prayed for comfort, and we shed a lot of tears. Our time of sharing was something I wouldn't trade for any amount of money or for

the promise of a thousand carefree moments. Was it fun? No.
But the growth we experienced was better than fun. This was
an opportunity to rely on the Lord in a way we'd never done
before.

Now, before we go on, we want to make one important distinction. We probably all know the experience of being blindsided by what we might call *impersonal* circumstances—tragedies like diseases and natural disasters that aren't caused by other people. Most of the examples of circumstantial wreckage in this chapter fall into this category.

But there's a separate category that we call *relational* circumstances. These are happenings we don't choose or control that are caused by other people. They result from someone else's decisions or sins.

Both types of circumstances hurt. But the ways we process them and heal from them are very different. With impersonal circumstances, we go more quickly to the question of God's role. We wonder if He's paying attention, since it seems like a loving Father would protect His children from suffering. Our struggle is one of faith, of striving to believe that even in the midst of suffering God is good and He's there for us.

In contrast, we process suffering caused directly by other people less philosophically; it feels more tangible. A particular person or group did something stupid or hurtful; we can easily identify and blame someone for the consequences we have to endure. With this kind of wreckage, one of our biggest challenges is forgiveness, and in some cases reconciliation.

But in both kinds of circumstances, sooner or later we wonder why God allowed it to happen. *It just isn't fair.* And we're always faced with a basic question: Who do I believe God really is in the face of tragedy?

Where Did God Go?

Job felt completely abandoned by God. He knew God existed in heaven. (After all, he'd spent much of the book talking to God.) And he never really blamed God. But he felt a desolate distance between him and God, a total isolation from God. And that didn't make sense. So he voiced his perplexity, sometimes in harsh terms:

> I loathe my very life; therefore I will give free rein to my complaint and speak out in the bitterness of my soul.

> I will say to God: Do not condemn me, but tell me what charges you have against me.

> Does it please you to oppress me, to spurn the work of your hands, while you smile on the schemes of the wicked?[9]

In his despair, Job wished he had never been born. *God, where are You?* alternated with *God, why are You*

9 Job 10:1-3

destroying me? If you've ever fallen victim to tragic circumstances, you can probably identify.

[Toben] *When I was diagnosed with bipolar disorder, I was devastated. Mental illness was one of the worst problems I could imagine. I knew nothing about bipolar and assumed that for the rest of my life I would feel as bad as I felt at that moment. It didn't help that the first few months of drug therapy made me worse, not better. I remember clearly the desperation, the anxiety, the hopelessness. They pervaded my soul.*

I needed someone to blame, so I walked away from God. This type of disorder isn't really anybody's fault, so there's no one to get mad at. (Well, I actually got mad at a lot of people, but not for any valid reasons.) So I went after God . . . by going away from God. On the rare occasions when I went to church with my family, I felt like I was suffocating. My chest would tighten and my ears would buzz during the worship times. I felt on the verge of panic. Visits to the bathroom were often my excuse for escape.

For a year I avoided church. I didn't pray. I didn't sing. I didn't touch a Bible. I didn't listen to Christian bands. Christianity and I weren't on speaking terms.

Many people in the midst of circumstantial wreckage find themselves reevaluating their relationship with God. Of course we ask why. We tell God off. We ask God if He's still up there. If He still cares. The book of Job is included in the Bible to show us that we're not the first ones to ask God tough questions. And we won't be the last.

Even more comforting is the freedom in knowing that God is okay with our questions. He's big enough to handle them. In fact, it's even possible for us to ask our honest questions . . . without sinning! Job did. Scripture says that throughout his suffering he never sinned against God. Yes, he complained bitterly, but God was patient with his honest expression of emotions—even the inaccurate perceptions he voiced about God.

The key was that he expressed himself with honesty and reverence. And he kept turning to God as the only possible source of restoration rather than turning to destructive substitute behaviors. Job's example teaches us that it's possible to suffer terribly and voice our feelings and thoughts honestly to God without sinning against Him.

Some Friends!

Much of the book of Job consists of advice from Job's friends—Bildad, Eliphaz, Zophar, and Elihu. Can you say *long-winded?* Most of their well-intended guidance for Job was less than helpful. The one thing they did right was to sit with Job silently for seven days, struck by the depth of Job's suffering. Once Job broke the silence, his friends refused to shut up for the next thirty or so chapters. They should have kept quiet. Of course Job had a thing or two to say, but his friends out-worded him in their attempts to "help."

Their central message? *Job, buddy, admit it. You sinned, didn't you? Otherwise God wouldn't be punishing you like this.*

Job's consistent response: *I've done nothing wrong. I have no idea why this is happening, but I've lived an upright life before God.*

Back and forth they went, until the first three friends had exhausted themselves, unable to persuade Job. That's when Elihu stepped in (see Job 32–37). His argument is summed up in 34:11: "[God] repays a man for what he has done; he brings upon him what his conduct deserves." In other words, *Job, you got what you had coming. God is just and wouldn't be putting you through this if you were as morally upright as you say you are.* Same song, second verse.

Now, we can't fault these guys' motives. At least they showed up, right? But their original plan was best—just *sitting* with Job. Don't forget, all this time, Job was covered head to foot with terrible, oozing sores and was grieving his family and sudden poverty. He was in pain—both physically and emotionally—and now he had to argue his case against the relentless accusations of his friends besides.

One of the secondary burdens that comes with circumstantial wreckage is friends or acquaintances who think they know exactly what we need to do. And they're not afraid to tell us. Usually they really want to help, but most of the time it feels condescending or judgmental, or at least demonstrates a lack of understanding and empathy.

[Ryan] *I got a lot of this in connection with my divorce. My "favorite" line was, "Ryan, God is doing this for a reason! He's doing this to prepare you for something in the future." Inside, I thought,* Man, if that's true, what a cruel, cruel joke. Thanks, but no thanks. *I just wanted an easy life, a good marriage, someone who loved me who I could love. At the time I was overwhelmed with the death of that dream; I didn't care about anything else in the future.*

What I needed most, at least in the early stages of my pain, were people who would just stand by me while I processed my emotions. Mainly just listening and showing they understood. They didn't even have to agree with me; I just needed to be free to be myself with them, to be real with them.

Eventually I was able to accept the reality that God had allowed suffering and pain and wreckedness in my life for good reasons, even if I couldn't see those reasons yet. I came to realize that He would somehow use my divorce—and all the other bad stuff that happened to me—for my good and His purposes (see Romans 8:28-30).

I knew I had a choice to make: I could be bitter toward God or I could believe that He would use my tragedy for greater good. One friend told me, "Bitterness is like swallowing poison and waiting for someone else to die." That's what I was doing. So I puked up the poison.

God didn't cause my divorce, but He did allow it to happen. And I've come to a place where I'm okay with Him allowing that. I don't have to understand all His reasons; what really

112

matters is putting myself trustingly in His hands (where I've actually been all along). I've chosen not to let my situation shake my faith or taint what I know to be true of God. I choose to follow Him freely and willingly.

There's no way we can jump directly to this place of calm, truthful acceptance of our life-wrecking circumstances. *They hurt!* And there's no way past the pain except to walk through it. While we're hurting, we need shoulders to cry on, arms to hold us, ears to listen to our irrational rantings. When the pain is fresh, we're too weak to handle too many heavy teachings or trite sayings.

But the time comes when we must face . . .

God's Questions

Finally, after Job and his friends had their say, God spoke. And when He did, He left no room for discussion! We'll get into what He said in a minute, but first notice that God *did* respond. Do you think Job actually expected the heavens to open and God to answer him? Doubtful. More likely God's voice came as a shock. In Job 38:2-3, as elsewhere in Scripture, God spoke out of a storm, immediately setting the tone:[10]

Who is this that darkens my counsel with words without knowledge? Brace yourself like a man; I will question you, and you shall answer me.

---

10 See 2 Samuel 22:10-16; Psalm 50:3; Isaiah 30:30; and Nahum 1:3.

When God broke through, Job was completely absorbed in his own problems. And understandably so, considering all he'd endured without apparent cause. But as surprised as Job must have been when God spoke, he was probably even more surprised that God got right in his face. After all, poor Job was still covered in sores. And his life, as far as he could tell, was completely and permanently wrecked.

What God proceeded to say was, in effect: "I'm God, and you're not." Period. Of course, He took three chapters to expand on His central thesis. But the upshot is clear: God is in control, and Job, for all his problems, was relatively insignificant in the scheme of history and eternity.

Wouldn't you think a loving God would have struck a more conciliatory tone? "Wow, Job, I'm really sorry for all of this, but I'll make it up to you. Really." Nope. Although God did eventually replace all Job had lost, and more, He never directly answered any of Job's questions. Instead, He responded with some questions of His own—questions that put Job squarely in his place. Here are a few of our favorites:

Will the one who contends with the Almighty correct him? Let him who accuses God answer him!

Can you pull in the leviathan [some huge sea creature] with a fishhook or tie down his tongue with a rope?

Who then is able to stand against me? Who has a claim against me that I must pay? Everything under heaven belongs to me.[11]

Job's response? Dumbstruck silence. He jumps in only once with a brief response in chapter 40: "I am unworthy—how can I reply to you? I put my hand over my mouth. I spoke once, but I have no answer—twice, but I will say no more" (Job 40:4-5). God's point (and ours) is that despite how big our problems seem, no matter how wrecked we are, no matter how justified our self-focus might seem, He is still God. Yes, we can question Him, we can get mad at Him, and we can turn away from Him, but that doesn't change Him. It only changes us.

There's something to be said for the constancy of God. Sometimes it's frustrating, like when we're looking for loopholes in truth or when we want God to seem more politically correct. But when we're willing to trust Him, we find relief in knowing that God is always the same, no matter what our circumstances. And we find encouragement in seeing the true size of our problems in light of God's immensity.

[Ryan] *When I was in the middle of my divorce and my life was completely upside down, I found solace in one activity—surfing. I honestly believe God gave me surfing as a personal gift during that time. I had tried it maybe once or twice before,*

11 Job 40:2; Job 41:1; Job 41:10-11

and now a friend kept inviting me to go surfing with him and some friends.

I'm not a great surfer. But I love it. Because when I'm in the ocean, I feel closest to God—especially when the ocean rears up and throws serious waves at the shore. I can visually see my insignificance compared to the world around me. More than that, I pause in amazement that the God who created these waves, tides, dolphins, and everything else . . . knows me by name. He knows me intimately and cares for me. He graces me with experiences and pictures that demonstrate His power, His majesty, and His love.

In those surfing moments I was reminded that the ocean is very, very big. And in the presence of its bigness, I realized that I am very, very small. More often than not, especially on those big days, the ocean would pummel me. It would knock me down, throw me under, and spin me around like a rag doll. It would hold me down until I thought my lungs would burst, until I would rise to the surface and gasp for my next breath. This helped me gain a proper perspective on God—His awesome power reflected in His creation—and on myself.

As big as my problems seemed, they were small in comparison to the wide world God created. I would also be reminded about other people around the world who weren't living in a sun-kissed California beach town—those who really suffered, every day, and had to fight just to survive. The ocean became my metaphor for God's bigness. And in that metaphor, my proper place was framed. Even when my problems came

*crashing down, overwhelming me, I knew that my easiest path
back into God's presence was a short trip to the beach.*

God speaks, and He does so in different ways. Sometimes quietly, sometimes loudly; sometimes through
friends, and other times through nature. God can speak
to us through a book or a preacher or His Word. And when
we're wrecked by circumstance, even if we lash out and
make arrogant demands of Him, He's there, unchanging,
so much bigger and more powerful than our problems.
And so willing to care.

Are You Listening?

Job's suffering ended with a clear message from God and
an immediate change of circumstances. Wouldn't it be
nice if all our tragedies ended this way? Maybe one of
yours has, but we've all been around the block enough
times to know that hearing God's voice clearly in difficult
situations isn't a common experience.

Still, God *does* speak.

117

[Toben] *In my case, as I was struggling to accept and adapt
to my bipolar disorder, God spoke very, very quietly. And for
months I didn't hear Him because the noise in my brain was
so loud. I can't point to a specific day or moment when I heard
Jesus' still, small voice. I tuned Him in gradually over time,
over days and weeks and months.*

I do remember what the voice said: "Stop running." That was it.

"Running from what?" I shouted back at God.

He simply said . . . "Stop running."

After a couple of months I finally figured out what He meant. And then things changed.

What He meant was that striving toward Him or away from Him wasn't going to make Him love me any more or any less. I had always believed that I needed to run toward God all the time, and that if I didn't, I wasn't much of a Christian. And I, being one for action, figured that if I wasn't moving toward God, I might as well run away from Him. I wasn't aware that some of the most devout Christians sometimes just stand still in God's presence. They let Him do the moving.

Everything else in my life was total chaos. God was telling me to stop moving. To stop trying to create my own meaning or solutions in my life. I was making it worse. He wanted me to stand still, to allow Him to come to me where I was, and to let Him minister to me.

God actually used a human voice to tell me this. I was on the phone with my friend Jonathan one day. I was standing in my backyard recounting what a mess my life felt like. Then Jonathan said something that stuck with me and serves me well to this day. He said, "Toben, God loves you enough to come after you. And He loves you enough to not let you get away from Him. He's going to pursue you no matter where you go."

Those words rocked me, because they lent a physical voice to that still, small voice that had been trying to break

through. I got the picture. Still, this was a theological challenge for me because I had never really thought God loved
me that much.

I wrestled to begin accepting God's love, and things started
to change. My suffering didn't end instantly, but my soul
became less raw, less wounded. My meds got straightened
out, and my brain finally got quiet. My anxiety lessened its
grip, and my relationships began the long, slow process of
healing. Everything didn't get better the way it did for Job, but
my life after the bipolar diagnosis is better than before. Those
who know me know I'm no Pollyanna, but I can honestly say
that everything I went through—all that suffering and self-
destruction and self-medication—was worth it for what God
has done in my life as a result.

[Ryan] *This may sound strange, but I actually heard God's
audible voice. During my darkest time in the midst of my
divorce, my friend Joe White, the president of Kanakuk Kamps,
called me and invited me to spend some time at his camp. I
politely declined. I was thirty years old and in the middle of
a crisis. The last thing I needed was camp! But I kept hearing
voices urging me to reconsider. Not God's voice, but my dad's
and Joe's. Looking back, I realize they were speaking God's
words to me, but it wasn't until later that I heard God's voice
directly.*

*I finally relented and spent a month at Joe's camp. I hadn't
really listened to God in more than five years. I was mad. Mad
at my failed and miserable marriage, mad at my job, mad*

*at my lack of friends, mad that I didn't have a good church.
Mostly I was mad at God because He'd let all this happen
to me.*

*A young camp counselor we called "Cowboy" became my
friend. This guy absolutely poured himself into the Bible. He
would prop it up on his steering wheel and read while driving
(not something I recommend!). One morning I was sitting on
the dock with another counselor named Matt when Cowboy
walked up and announced that God had spoken to him the
night before and had given him a verse for me. To be honest, I didn't listen to Cowboy's verse. I was too busy asking
cynically, in my head, why God hadn't given the verse to me
Himself.*

*After Cowboy walked away, I voiced my cynical question to
Matt. He replied, "Maybe He did and you weren't listening." A
bomb exploded in my head. I went back to my cabin that night
and read the verse myself. It was then I actually heard God's
voice. I may sound like a crazy person; I don't care. I just sat
there and listened. He told me many things, but what stuck
with me the most was that (1) He would be there with me every
step of the way, and (2) I must be obedient to Him. It was His
way or the highway.*

*My problems didn't go away; in fact, they got a whole lot
worse in the next year. But every step of the way I knew God
was by my side. I stopped trusting my instincts and feelings
and started doing what God was asking of me. Since that
time He has never left my side (not that He had before), and I
haven't stopped listening. Certainly there have been times I've*

blown it and done my own thing, but now I'm trying to point my life in His direction and not my own.

For Job, the turning point came when he listened to God. Everything he'd lost came back to him. No doubt he continued to endure sadness over the death of his children. And since he was a caring man, he must also have grieved over his slaughtered servants. But after hearing from God, Job went on with a clearer understanding of God and of himself.

Our hope is that you'll gain this understanding too. If you've gone through extreme circumstances in the past, we pray that God is leading you through the aftermath to a better, fuller life . . . that God is redeeming your crisis. If you are wrecked by circumstances at this moment, hold out hope that God is speaking, that you can hear Him, and that He will lead you into a fuller life.

And if you have yet to endure any serious suffering, try to cement these principles in your brain . . . because pain happens. Things go wrong—sometimes terribly so. Remember the experiences of Job, and remember that there is hope. Read and reflect on Scripture. Come face-to-face with God regularly; grow to know Him well.

Then when life happens to you, you'll be securely, confidently tied to Him, already tapping into His infinite resources.

The Wrecked Life: Obedience

— — —

Who wants to follow Jesus? Yes, I see that hand. And I see that hand in the front. And over there on the left, love your enthusiasm. Thank you.

Walking life's road with Jesus is wonderful, isn't it? Think about it. He promised, "Come to me . . . and I will give you rest," and "My yoke is easy to bear, and the burden I give you is light" (Matthew 11:28, 30, NLT). Psalm 23 paints a picture of still waters and green pastures. And if those weren't enough, imagine what it means that we can "keep on asking, and you will receive what you ask for" (Matthew 7:7, NLT), for Pete's sake!

Oh, but wait a minute. There is also that thing about the valley of the shadow of death in Psalm 23. And Jesus did preach, "In this world you will have trouble" (John 16:33). And He said, "All men will hate you because of me" (Luke 21:17). Hebrews 11:36-37 describes a reality involving jeering and whippings, and obedient people who were "chained and put in prison . . . stoned . . . sawed in two . . . put to death by the sword." In fact, come to think of it, the Bible doesn't have many stories about people who followed Christ and had an easy go of it.

Reality check! We Jesus followers like to pick out the nice, pleasant parts of the obedient life. But nowhere in the Bible are we guaranteed that life with Christ will be easy, carefree . . . ordinary. In fact, we're guaranteed the opposite—that following Jesus will mean a wrecked life for sure, at least by the world's standards. Just about all the people in the Old and New Testaments lived some sort of wrecked life because they obeyed God. Think about Noah, Gideon, David, any of the prophets, and the disciples. They all had crazy, upside-down lives. They were "good wrecked." Wrecked *because* they did it God's way.

"Wait a minute," you say. "Are you suggesting that God purposely calls us to wrecked lives? That's not what I signed up for when I got on board with faith."

Honestly? Yes, that's exactly what we're suggesting. That's the life that Jesus invites His true disciples to be part of . . . and expect. And He didn't hide it in the fine print.

So far in this book we've talked about wrecked lives that result from our own sinful choices or from circumstances we can't control. But your life can also feel smashed and obliterated when you do what God says. Obedience might make you look like a total fool to everyone around you; your life might look like a complete wreck. Even *you* might feel like you're signing on to ruin your life.

Look at the ultimate wrecked life: Christ Himself. He of all people knew exactly what was going on while He lived here, and sometimes He must have felt devastated, damaged beyond repair. For the first thirty or so years of His life, He seems to have had a fairly normal existence as a carpenter. Then God called Him into action, and any semblance of "comfortable" or "ordinary" became mere memories. He was baptized by John the Baptist, and His Father's voice from heaven said, "This is my Son, whom I love; with him I am well pleased" (Matthew 3:17). Immediately after that, God's Spirit led Him into the wilderness to be tempted by the devil. Eventually Jesus' path led to torture and finally to a brutal death on the cross.

Behold your Leader. The One you say you're following. If His wasn't a wrecked life, whose is?

If God intended to call His followers to "normal" lives, wouldn't that be modeled in Scripture, particularly in the life of His own Son? Don't you think we'd see a picture of a less radical, more laid-back, comfortable Jesus?

Yet somehow, not one of the people who led wrecked lives for the sake of God's Kingdom would have traded it for anything. In the midst of the wreckage, they experienced power and blessings that made their circumstances seem worthwhile. Just listen to the apostle Paul in 2 Corinthians 11:23-28:

> I have worked much harder, been in prison more frequently, been flogged more severely, and been exposed to death again and again. Five times I received from the Jews the forty lashes minus one. Three times I was beaten with rods, once I was stoned, three times I was shipwrecked, I spent a night and a day in the open sea, I have been constantly on the move. I have been in danger from rivers, in danger from bandits, in danger from my own countrymen, in danger from Gentiles; in danger in the city, in danger in the country, in danger at sea; and in danger from false brothers. I have labored and toiled and have often gone without sleep; I have known hunger and thirst and have often gone without food; I have been cold and naked. Besides everything else, I face daily the pressure of my concern for all the churches.

Quite a list! At any point, Paul could have given up. He could have retired and lived out his life in peace and quiet. But he felt compelled to something more as described in 2 Corinthians 6:4-10 (*The Message*):

> Our work as God's servants gets validated—or not—in the details. People are watching us as we stay

at our post, alertly, unswervingly . . . in hard times,
tough times, bad times; when we're beaten up, jailed,
and mobbed; working hard, working late, working
without eating; with pure heart, clear head, steady
hand; in gentleness, holiness, and honest love; when
we're telling the truth, and when God's showing his
power; when we're doing our best setting things
right; when we're praised, and when we're blamed;
slandered, and honored; true to our word, though
distrusted; ignored by the world, but recognized by
God; terrifically alive, though rumored to be dead;
beaten within an inch of our lives, but refusing to die;
immersed in tears, yet always filled with deep joy;
living on handouts, yet enriching many; having nothing, having it all.

Having nothing, but having it all. It doesn't get much
clearer than that. Paul had nothing (according to the
world's opinion) and suffered greatly, but he considered
himself fortunate—he claimed to have it all! All of God's
eternal riches.

How backward from the way most of us think. If we
found ourselves in Paul's position, would we be able to
say the same thing? Or would we feel abandoned by God?
Would we agree that the reward is worth the cost?

Paul affirmed in words and actions that a life wrecked
by obedience to Christ is as good as it gets. It's the best life
we can hope for while we walk this earth. Yet how many of

us would measure our success or joy by laying out a port-folio like Paul's?

In Philippians 4:12-13, Paul said, "I know what it is to be in need, and I know what it is to have plenty. I have learned the secret of being content in any and every situation, whether well fed or hungry, whether living in plenty or in want. I can do everything through him who gives me strength." We all go through calm seasons and wrecked seasons. A normal life now doesn't guarantee it'll be that way forever, and a wrecked life now doesn't imply nothing will ever change for the better. Whatever our lives look like at the moment, we need to remain alert for whatever's coming next.

[Toben] *A few years ago I came into contact with four guys from Westmont College who were intentional about living lives of wrecked obedience. These guys were doing the usual college thing—attending classes and hanging out with their friends. But then during their senior year, they got a big idea from God that turned their lives upside down. God called them to travel around the world—literally—and do missions work with various groups for an entire year. So they did. They raised money, made plans, and set out after graduation. Over that year they served in a half-dozen different countries and communities with people in full-time missions work. When I spent time with them, it was obvious that their lives had been deeply and permanently affected by their experiences.*

I'm not sure what happened to these guys; we haven't

stayed in touch. I imagine that at least a couple of them have returned to "normal" lives. But I also imagine that they're all open to the possibility of some amazing, unpredictable adventure, something that changes their life direction and takes them off on an entirely different course. The four guys I knew were sold out, ready to let God wreck them for His glory.

When we're wrecked as a result of answering God's call, we learn about God's character. We also learn what we're capable of, what we can withstand, and what blessings lie at the end of obedience, even in the midst of pain.

When we're willing to lean into and learn from the wreckage, we experience a closer relationship with God. We build a new, more personal reliance on Christ as we trust Him for strength to obey. Through the tough stuff, He transforms our flaws and deficiencies.

Calling All Disciples

As Jesus was walking beside the Sea of Galilee, he saw two brothers, Simon called Peter and his brother Andrew. They were casting a net into the lake, for they were fishermen. "Come, follow me," Jesus said, "and I will make you fishers of men." At once they left their nets and followed him.

Going on from there, he saw two other brothers, James son of Zebedee and his brother John. They

were in a boat with their father Zebedee, preparing
their nets. Jesus called them, and immediately they
left the boat and their father and followed him.[12]

What *isn't* Matthew saying in this story? It seems a little
too easy. What are we left to imagine between the lines?

Here were a bunch of fishermen minding their own
business, and out of nowhere Jesus showed up. The disciples had likely heard something about Jesus, but probably
not much. Maybe the story of His baptism and God's voice
from the sky. But not much more had happened yet.

You see, Jesus was still at the very front end of His
ministry. He probably didn't have a long résumé of accomplishments that He could lay out to entice these fishermen
to follow Him. In retrospect, we can see the full picture of
Jesus as the Son of God and as the fulfillment of centuries
of prophecy. But for those early disciples, the story was
still being written; Jesus called them before He became
"famous."

In fact, the Israelites hadn't heard directly from God
for hundreds of years. Many of the Jews assumed that the
days of direct revelation had passed. Most who heeded
the abundance of prophecy about the coming Messiah
expected a powerful military leader, not a carpenter/
teacher. Many others had given up even watching for the
Messiah. So when Jesus showed up, most people weren't
expecting Him.

But Jesus' lack of a résumé didn't stop the first disciples

from responding to His call. When Jesus asked Simon Peter and Andrew to drop everything and follow Him . . . they did! A freak occurrence? Maybe Peter and Andrew were bored with fishing and had already been thinking about a career change. Uh, don't think so. A little later it happened *again*! Jesus called James and John. They dropped everything, left their dad to mind the sloop, and followed Jesus.

Rob Bell, the founding pastor of Mars Hill Bible Church in Grandville, Michigan, also makes short films. (If you haven't heard of NOOMA, stop reading and go to nooma. com now!) In the short film *Dust*, Rob says, "If they're fishermen and Jesus calls them to be his disciples, then they're not following another rabbi; and if they're not following another rabbi, then they're not the best of the best. They didn't make the cut."

Rob explains that Jewish boys in Jesus' day were separated into two groups—the really smart ones and the average ones. The average ones ended their schooling at about nine or ten and went out into the workplace to learn a trade. The smart ones continued their schooling, and the best of these were taken on as apprentices to rabbis. They would become disciples of a rabbi and learn everything he could possibly teach them. This was considered among the highest of honors. Parents of these chosen young men no doubt plastered their donkey carts with stickers that proudly boasted, "My son is an honor student of Rabbi So-and-So."

But Jesus wasn't calling the best of the best. He was calling the ones who hadn't made the cut. They'd already been labeled second best. Or worse. Now they were being granted the honor they'd long ago stopped hoping for. What in the world was going on?

Regardless, Jesus called, and they followed—as unlikely as it might have seemed to the watching world.

Dropping Everything

It's easy for us today to say, "If Jesus called me like that, I would totally do it. I mean it's *Jesus*, right?" But we have two thousand years of history and a whole Bible full of information on who Jesus is, so we have a decided edge. To those first disciples, Jesus was an unknown. For all they knew, He was a crackpot. But something about Jesus must have drawn them. Maybe they were among the few who really read the Scriptures; they matched what they heard about Him with prophecies of the coming Son of God.

Still, think for a minute about what it meant for Peter, Andrew, James, and John to dump everything to follow Jesus. They had *lives*. Jobs, families, friends, homes. But in Mark 10:28-30 we read:

> Peter said to him, "We have left everything to follow you!"
>
> "I tell you the truth," Jesus replied, "no one who has left home or brothers or sisters or mother or father

or children or fields for me and the gospel will fail to receive a hundred times as much in this present age (homes, brothers, sisters, mothers, children and fields—and with them, persecutions) and in the age to come, eternal life."

At least some of the disciples were married and probably had children. These weren't unattached free-lancers finally cutting the apron strings, getting away from the nest to go on a wild adventure. They were leaving people, places, and possessions that meant everything to them. How many nights did they lie awake agonizing over their new, radical commitment? *We must be crazy to be following this guy. They were human. Everyone has their doubts.*

Yet they followed. They must have had their days when following Jesus was obviously the best decision they'd ever made. Jesus granted them amazing power, "authority to drive out evil spirits and to heal every disease and sickness" (Matthew 10:1). From manual laborers to miracle workers and exorcists. The disciples must have been most sold out when using Jesus' incredible gifts.

Even so, Jesus' followers paid an amazing price. The world watched and evaluated the wreckage that characterized their existence. Quality of life? Bad choice. Secure relationships? Bad choice. Life expectancy? Bad choice.

But we can see that they made the *best* choice!

Let's focus on one of Jesus' many wrecked followers:

Saul, who later became Paul. (See Acts 9 for more about his story.)

Saul had made the cut. He was among the Jewish elite, the best of the best. A famous rabbi named Gamaliel had taken him on as an honored disciple, granting Saul automatic VIP status for life. Now some men in Saul's position would have used their advantage to cultivate a life of comfort and ease. But Saul didn't sit back and let life happen to him. He was zealous, and he showed it by running around persecuting those "heretics" who followed the false prophet Jesus. He was good at his job and probably earned more kudos from the Jewish establishment every time he threw a Christian in prison or had one executed.

Saul was on a seek-and-destroy mission to Damascus when Jesus interrupted his journey. Jesus appeared, surrounded by brilliant light, and said, "Saul, why are you persecuting me?"

Saul was blinded for several days. Even after he regained his sight, his encounter with Jesus proved to be, to all appearances, the destruction of his dreams. Such a promising young man, and here he was following Jesus. Immediately things got worse. Some Jewish leaders tried to kill the traitor, but Saul escaped to Jerusalem. There he faced further trouble: Jesus' disciples were afraid of him and refused to trust him (small wonder). Saul began to preach openly anyway, proclaiming Jesus as Lord and Messiah. He debated the Grecian Jews . . . and they tried to kill him too!

Saul's life was shredded to pieces and then thrown to the wind. He gave up his old identity—everything that had been important to him. His old friends were putting out contracts on his life. He tried to do the right thing, but his new friends wouldn't trust him. He was left with no choice but to travel from city to city, his life constantly on the line.

From a worldly perspective, Saul's bad decisions cost him his job, his reputation, his friends. The authorities who had been grooming him for leadership were baffled by his choice to go from persecutor to persecuted. And Saul's life never got any easier. He was imprisoned, beat up, and likely martyred.

But he became a pillar of the church. Many of us who are Jesus followers today can thank Saul (later Paul) for taking the news of Jesus to the world, to those who eventually passed the message down to us. He even wrote a significant chunk of the New Testament. In the world's view, obedience ruined Saul's life. But from our view—God's view—we know that obedient wreckage was Saul's best option.

The key factor in all of this is faith—faith that this decision to follow Christ, which flies in the face of reason, is the best decision we can make.

Culture is shouting, "Step away from the Christ. Run! You've got a stable life . . . a job, family, friends. What does this Jesus have to offer?"

135

And yet something inside says, "Take this path anyway; it leads to the best life."

And that's what Jesus always promised—not an easy life, just the best one.

[Ryan] *Let me tell you about one of my best friends, Jonathan. He used to be lead singer in a band. This guy is ridiculously talented—amazing voice and unmatched guitar skills. His band was well on its way to making it big. They were being flown back and forth from Los Angeles to New York to meet with various labels and producers.*

But the closer they came to a deal, the worse Jonathan felt. He kept getting the sense that this wasn't where God was leading him. The deal finally came to the table; their dream was within reach. That's when, according to Jonathan, he received another offer from God. He felt that God was calling him away from a music career and into ministry. What to do?

The music deal meant unimaginable money, concert tours, a nice house, flashy cars, and all the rest. If he took God's deal, he was signing up for very little money (Jonathan had five kids at the time), no insurance, and a mortgage. Plus, he'd be letting down the rest of the band. Pile on top of that the pressure of all the people who couldn't understand why he was even considering wrecking his life.

As I write this, Jonathan is on a road trip with his five kids (and pregnant wife) from Colorado to Mississippi, where he will be a guest preacher for the next several weeks.

Saying Yes

We have advantages today that the disciples didn't have. A complete picture of the person and purpose of Jesus. And the Holy Spirit living and moving in us.

We have our disadvantages, too. How many of us have faced tough decisions and wished that Jesus would show up in person and tell us the right thing to do? Yet God speaks to us. Subtly, quietly. But unmistakably. Our job is to listen carefully. And when we hear His still, small voice prompting us to act, we will never regret saying yes. How often have each of us ignored a nudge from God and later wished we hadn't! When God commands, He expects one thing: compliance.

[Toben] *For much of my adult life, when I saw homeless people I would just pass by. I don't know why exactly, but I always excused myself: I'm in a hurry; I only have large bills; he'll probably use it to buy alcohol. But every time I did that, I'd feel a little knot in my stomach, a twinge that something wasn't quite right.*

It was Joanne who got my attention one day. She announced that she was no longer going to ignore the homeless. She was going to give . . . and engage. I decided to follow her lead.

We often see a couple of homeless guys near the exit to our girls' school. I'm no saint, believe me. But when those men are there, I stop and talk to them, I give them what I have (which sometimes really hurts), and I drive away without that knot, that twinge. Listening to that little voice is part of obeying God and letting Him wreck my life—someday maybe in a big way, often just a little bit at a time.

Not long ago we met a group of twentysomethings from a ministry called International Justice Mission (ijm. org), a human rights agency that assists victims of violence, sexual exploitation, slavery, and oppression in poor countries around the world. Two members of this group had Oxford law degrees, another had graduated summa cum laude in English, and another had a University of Southern California premed degree. All were smart, hardworking, and positioned for great success.

But they were all working for IJM as *unpaid interns.* Let that sink in. Well-educated graduates with decades of opportunity ahead of them. Any one of them could have done just about anything he or she wanted. But they chose to work for free for an organization they believed in.

Their friends who had pursued advanced degrees or gone to work for good money didn't get it. Their families struggled to understand why, after spending hundreds of thousands on their educations, they would work for nothing.

They seemed to be blowing their futures, wrecking their lives. Did they have regrets? Not a one.

These individuals said yes with their wealth, their careers, their opportunities. And around the world, a large and growing number of Jesus followers are called to say yes to God with their very lives. We hear stories about heroes throughout history who were martyred in obedience to Christ. But in our time, more Christians are tortured and killed for their faith each year than ever before. The number grows annually.

Ling, for example, is a Chinese believer who was caught with Bibles and other Christian materials in his home. The authorities discovered that the books and videos were being produced inside China. They intimidated and pressured Ling to reveal who else was involved and where the materials were being produced. But Ling refused to dishonor His heavenly Father and His fellow believers. We won't go into details, but Ling came to be known as "the one who got his fingernails taken." He was imprisoned for three years in a "reeducation through labor" camp, where he was beaten and tortured. When he was released in 2004, he joyfully returned to his calling, spreading the life-giving truth of Jesus to others in his country.[13] Ling has tasted what it is to be "good wrecked," and he counts it as a privilege to suffer for his obedience.

Gideon's Yes

One of our favorite yes-men (in a good sense of the term) was a guy named Gideon. (His story can be found in Judges 6–7.)

Here's the backstory: The Israelites had offended God, and for seven years he "handed [them] over to the

---

13 Ling's story is adapted from Voice of the Martyrs (www.persecution.com), as excerpted from Randy Alcorn's Eternal Perspective Ministries Web site (www.epm.org/articles/chinesebrothers_story.html).

Midianites." These Midianites were not nice people, and the Israelites took to living in caves in the hills for fear of them. The Midianites routinely destroyed their crops and stole their animals—everything Israel needed to live.

Israel called out to God for relief, and after seven years an angel (actually the Lord) appeared to young Gideon.

> The LORD turned to him and said, "Go in the strength you have and save Israel out of Midian's hand. Am I not sending you?"
>
> "But LORD," Gideon asked, "how can I save Israel? My clan is the weakest in Manasseh, and I am the least in my family."
>
> The LORD answered, "I will be with you, and you will strike down all the Midianites together."[14]

We guess that by now Gideon was freaking out. And cynical. The Lord's reference to him as a mighty warrior must have rung false in Gideon's ears. So Gideon tested the Lord: "If you are truly going to help me, show me a sign to prove that it is really the Lord speaking to me."[15] He prepared an offering of bread and meat and set it on a rock, and at the angel's directive the bread and meat were consumed by fire.

Gideon got the point—this angel was for real. So now

14 Judges 6:14-16
15 Judges 6:17, NLT

that he had Gideon's attention, the angel said: "Do not be afraid. You will not die."[16]

Notice that the angel didn't say, "Don't worry; things are going to be easy." He only said fatality wasn't on the horizon in the near future.

We jump ahead to see Gideon test the Lord again. He laid out a sheepskin and requested God to make the sheepskin wet and leave everything around it dry. God did that. Then Gideon tested God again! This time, Gideon wanted the fleece to be dry and everything else wet. God did that too.

So Gideon gave God the benefit of the doubt and decided to believe Him. (Duh. Good call.)

Gideon gathered an army and set out to beat up on the Midianites. But . . .

> The LORD said to Gideon, "You have too many men for me to deliver Midian into their hands. In order that Israel may not boast against me that her own strength has saved her, announce now to the people, 'Anyone who trembles with fear may turn back and leave Mount Gilead.'" So twenty-two thousand men left, while ten thousand remained.

> But the LORD said to Gideon, "There are still too many men. Take them down to the water, and I will sift them for you there. If I say, 'This one shall go with

you,' he shall go; but if I say, 'This one shall not go with you,' he shall not go."

So Gideon took the men down to the water. There the LORD told him, "Separate those who lap the water with their tongues like a dog from those who kneel down to drink." Three hundred men lapped with their hands to their mouths. All the rest got down on their knees to drink.

The LORD said to Gideon, "With the three hundred men that lapped I will save you and give the Midianites into your hands. Let all the other men go, each to his own place." So Gideon sent the rest of the Israelites to their tents but kept the three hundred, who took over the provisions and trumpets of the others.[17]

Make sure you get this right: Gideon started out with thirty-two thousand men. God left him with three hundred. One little problem. The Midianites were as "thick as locusts," and their camels were as numerous as the sand on the beach. Not quite the odds Gideon was hoping for. God wrecked Gideon's army! And Gideon was tempted to fear that he himself would be next for demolition.

Without getting into all the details, let's just say that Gideon and his men beat the tar out of the Midianites. And a man who considered himself a small, weak wreck but who was obedient even when it seemed crazy was transformed into a warrior and a leader.

Though terrified, Gideon eventually took every step God told him to take. But in the time it took for this to unfold, 31,700 men returned to their homes, confident that Gideon had lost his mind. Many of them must have told their families to expect a few more decades under the Midianites' thumb.

God proved His strength and was glorified when a man became both a wreck and a hero through his obedience.

Your Yes

Gideon's story isn't just some isolated, irrelevant, oddball legend. It's full of real-life lessons for us.

We can ask God for confirmation.

When God directs our paths, especially in the direction of wreckedness, it's okay to want a little validation for the message. Of course, we can't expect confirmation for every little decision. If you feel a gentle nudge to give a little something to a homeless person, you probably aren't going to get confirmation for that. (Parting with five bucks—or even a hundred—isn't going to wreck your life.) But if God is asking you to do something really risky, like leaving friends and family to serve far from home, God doesn't expect you to make that kind of sacrifice blindly; He'll make your way clear.

Now, be sure you make your confirmation request

with utmost humility. And go into it willing, if God directs and confirms, to do what He has called you to do. Gideon was skeptical but never belligerent or disrespectful. This was a huge decision; he just wanted a little support. And he got it.

When you question a message in humility, you're not questioning God. You're asking the God of the universe to show you that you weren't mistaken or fooled by some other sender.

What we're called to do may not make sense to us.
This is a tough one. We like to think that life has a certain order, that it's reasonable and logical. But Gideon's three-hundred-man army was totally *illogical*. If we require all of God's instructions to pass our standard of 100 percent rationality (to our minds), we'll limit our own faith in God's power, and He might not do everything He wants through us.

[Toben] *I work for a company that ministers to youth workers. If one thing has become clear to me over the years, it's that no one becomes a youth worker based on logic! It's an exhausting, 24-7 kind of job. The pay stinks. The elder board always has "issues." And the kids may or may not respond to one's best efforts.*

But I also know that youth workers are a passionate bunch. They love their kids and are willing to do just about anything to see young people give their lives to Christ and deepen their faith. Youth workers are called. They do it not because it makes a lot of sense but because God wants them to.

Keep in mind that God doesn't ask us to do something that may wreck our normal, everyday lives just because He can. He's a God of order; He issues every request and command for a good reason. God isn't in the business of jerking us around!

What we're called to do may not make sense to those around us.

Pink-slipping more than 99 percent of Gideon's army didn't make sense to the millions whose future depended on that army. People must have thought he was somewhere between nuts and suicidal.

Let's say God calls you to become homeless so you can better understand the plight of those folks. What will your family think? Or what if you take a year out of your life to serve in the poorest and most dangerous places in the world? What kinds of rumors will your neighbors pass around? Maybe you take your degree and use it, free of charge, to serve the oppressed. What judgments might you face from your friends?

God is glorified in our obedience.

God pared down Gideon's army so that the Israelites wouldn't get confused, thinking they'd won the battle by their strength. This was to be *God's* victory, and His alone. He had to be the obvious hero.

It's the same for us: God is glorified when we obey in the face of the impossible.

[Ryan] *Several years ago, I was working for a national youth ministry organization, handling all their tech support. I was also interning in the youth department of a large church in California. I was beginning to think about pursuing my public speaking career again. Years before, in college, I'd been called to preach the gospel to junior and senior high students. I seemed to hear God renewing that call.*

The problem was that I needed to be able to support a family, and speakers never know when the next check is coming. It's not a nine-to-five job with a predictable pay period. I wasn't sure I could make it as a speaker. So instead, I took a job in Washington, DC. It was my compromise with God . . . or so I thought. He'd called me to speak the gospel to youth; I took a job working on youth issues. We both win, right? Wrong.

Five years later, I was looking back and wondering what could have been if I had followed God. I'd sought counsel about going into speaking, but I just wasn't sure.

Then my world exploded. In the middle of my divorce, my contract with the youth organization ended. And due to my pending divorce, I was asked to terminate my internship with the church. I was sure the door to a speaking career was slamming in my face.

About that time the president of Ambassador Speakers Bureau, Wes Yoder, called and asked if I'd like to be represented by their agency. I didn't know what to say. Part of me wanted to jump at this incredible opportunity, but I also wondered if anyone would ever want me as a speaker. I explained my life situation to him. He thanked me for being honest and said he would get back to me.

I never expected to hear from him again. A few days later I left for Kanakuk, a remote camp in southwestern Missouri. I love Kanakuk for many reasons, but one of them is that it's so hard for anyone to contact me there. Sometimes it's nice to deny my cell phone addiction and just get lost. The only way for messages to get in is by mail. Snail mail. Only my parents and roommates knew where I was going.

At the camp I had the opportunity to speak to the students, and my heart ached to continue this ministry. My head told me I'd never get the chance.

Three weeks into my stay, I got a letter from Wes Yoder. It included a contract for representation and offers for my first three speaking events. How in the world he found me, I'll never know. This was confirmation from God—His way of telling me He'd never canceled His call on me. He was saying He wanted me to be His ambassador, sharing the gospel, even in the middle of my broken life.

I've been with the Ambassador agency for six years. I've spoken at hundreds of events and to hundreds of thousands of people of all ages.

I'm continually amazed that the Creator of all things has

147

chosen me. I have no idea how long this career will last or where it's taking me. But I know I'll follow as long as I'm able. If tomorrow the Lord asks me to give it all up and head to an unknown place, for an unknown time, with an unknown outcome, I'll follow. Seriously, how could I not? I know who I am, where I've been, and what I've gone through. God gave me my life back. How could I withhold anything from Him?

Everything I have is from God. Everything I've accomplished has been by His hand. The fact that He uses me is proof of His power.

Hearing God's Voice

Okay. We become completely committed to God. We have this gut-wrenching need to say yes to Him. How do we know what He's calling us to do?

God communicates with us in at least three tangible ways. If we're going to be wrecked by obedience, we have to know exactly what orders to obey. God makes His calling clear through Scripture, through other believers, and through the Holy Spirit.

The call through Scripture

If you want to know God's mind about something, a logical place to start is in the Book He's written. This won't work unless we're regularly spending time reading the Bible. Obvious, no? But we're prone to this crazy idea that when a challenge arises we can simply flip open the Bible and God will magically point us to the passage we need.

To be fair, that does happen sometimes, but it's not a method to count on. Instead, we read over and over in the Bible about our need to spend regular and consistent time studying God's Word (see Joshua 1:8; Psalms 1; 19; 119). And when we do, we make available one of the ways God can call us, prick our consciences, motivate us to change, and send us in new directions.

Reading Scripture is, in a real way, an ongoing discussion with God. Just as in a relationship with a friend, the good stuff comes over time. Trust and familiarity that grow over time make way for deeper interaction. It's in intimacy with God that the jewels of wisdom are communicated, sometimes when we least expect them!

149

[Toben] *This has happened to me most frequently with Chuck, my father-in-law. We can be hanging out, working on a project or sitting around the table after a meal. We can be talking about this or that, and then something he says turns a light on and shines truth into an area of my life. And I didn't even see it coming.*

It's the same with God's Word. Spending time with Him in the Bible creates opportunities for Him to turn on new lights for us.

Think about it like this: Suppose you had a friend you talked to only when you were in trouble. And you expected this person to always give you just the right advice at the right time. That would be unrealistic and unfair. It wouldn't be a relationship; it would be a transaction.

We need to immerse ourselves in Scripture—in God's heart—reading it as often as possible as an ongoing discussion, instead of using a hit-and-run approach.

[Toben] *Last December I was reading through Ephesians, and I came across this verse: "Do not let any unwholesome talk come out of your mouths, but only what is helpful for building others up according to their needs, that it may benefit those who listen" (4:29). It spoke to me in a specific way and called for a specific action.*

You see, I tended to be critical and cynical, and to occasionally use bad language. You may or may not think that's a big deal, but I felt God was calling me on it. This verse really connected with me, and I made a decision—a resolution—to live it out in my life. I still slip up and say things that aren't building anyone up. But listening—really listening—to God in Scripture and taking obedient action has made a tangible difference in the moments and days of my life.

God invites us into daily, intimate conversation in Scripture. Take Him up on it!

The call through other believers

Another way God shows us what direction to take—how to obey Him—is through the counsel of other believers. Paul's epistles are one clear example of God using a man to instruct the church in all matters spiritual and many matters practical, including divorce, marriage, parenting, and work. We may not have someone with Paul's horsepower in our lives, but chances are someone near us has walked the path a little longer or has some special wisdom and can offer us godly counsel.

[Ryan] *I'm a big believer in this. I do my best to surround myself with wise mentors and to listen to them as best I can. This was especially true after my divorce, when I started dating again. My parents lived several states away, so I didn't have them around to meet these women and give their opinions. That's where the Bengards, my second family, came in.*

I made a deal with the Bengards, a godly family whose insight I value, that I wouldn't go out with a girl more than three times before letting them meet her. They called it "Trial by Bengard." I called it "The Bengard Firing Squad." Their oldest son is a mixed martial arts fighter and trainer, so believe me when I say they don't pull any punches. The other part of the deal was, if they didn't approve of a girl, I had to break it off with her. They've really only liked one girl, and I'm happy to say that she's now my wife. But that's another story.

Shortly after meeting Laura, I knew she was the one I was going to marry. But still, I felt I needed the green light from the Bengards, my counselor, my friends, and my parents before I made any permanent decisions. So one after another, each of these people I respected met Laura and gave the thumbs-up. And she wasn't the only one who had to pass inspection. Soon I met her brothers and her parents, who all gave us their blessings.

My parents weren't an easy sell at first. My dad thought things were moving a little fast. Finally I told him, "Just meet her. If you think we aren't right for each other, tell me so, and I'll break it off."

We met the next night in Palm Springs. I've honestly never seen my mom take to someone so quickly. We'd no sooner walked through the door, than my mom took Laura by the arm to show her the condo they were thinking about buying. I looked at my dad questioningly. He just shrugged his shoulders. We all went to dinner, and on the way home my dad and mom gave us their blessings and prayed for us.

I knew this was a big decision and I needed to listen carefully for God's voice coming through godly people. And He came through, loud and clear.

The call through the Holy Spirit

The Holy Spirit, for many of us, can seem like the most challenging of these three means of communication to understand. Especially depending on the faith tradition we've grown up in or the church we attend. Maybe you can point to times when the Spirit has moved in you, giving you a gentle—or not so gentle—nudge to say or do something.

[Toben] *I remember sitting in a restaurant once, talking to a friend of a friend who wasn't a Christian. This guy was going*

through a tough time in his life, and I was trying to encour-
age him and share a little of my faith journey. I honestly
believe the Spirit took over and formed words for me. I said
things that I wasn't smart enough to say. I walked out of that
interaction knowing I'd heard God and obeyed His Holy Spirit
that day.

The Spirit does act and move in our lives. There's no set
formula here; He directs in whatever way He wants. If we
take the time to listen, the Holy Spirit's promptings can be
one of the ways we hear from God.

The Honor of Being Wrecked by Obedience

It's an honor to be wrecked by obedience. To receive God's
call and say yes.

But it may not *feel* like an honor at the time. The disciples' lives were wrecked by their obedience. They followed Jesus from town to town, with only the clothes on
their backs, not knowing what they'd eat or where they'd
sleep next. But the world now honors these first faithful
followers.

Think about paintings that aren't worth much when
the artist is alive, but whose value skyrockets after they
die. The same can be true for us. No one may recognize
or appreciate our obedient wreckage until much later—
maybe not even during our lifetimes.

We may receive one of the greatest joys of heaven when
we finally learn the value of our actions on earth. Maybe

we'll have something like a DVD library and we'll be able to watch the ways our little obediences multiplied into a huge impact in the lives we've touched.

[Toben] *One night I was flying to San Antonio, but bad weather forced the plane to land in Austin. I needed to rent a car to continue my journey, but by the time I got to the rental counter only one vehicle was left—a pickup truck. I turned to the guy in line behind me, also stranded, and invited him to split the cost and ride with me. He accepted.*

As we drove through a blinding rainstorm, he chain-smoked with the window barely cracked. After exchanging pleasantries, we got to talking about spiritual things. It was one of those times when I felt God prompting me to share the gospel. I worried that I might look foolish or that I might even stir up hostilities that I'd have to endure for two more hours. But I shared my faith.

Honestly, it didn't go that well. He was pretty resistant as he laid out his own beliefs, influenced largely by the movie The Last Temptation of Christ. *Not exactly a biblical view.*

We parted company with a handshake at the San Antonio airport and never saw each other again.

I have no idea if the conversation had any impact whatsoever. I don't expect to know until I get to heaven. But I felt—and still feel today—profoundly honored to have been granted the opportunity. I felt uncomfortable and I'm sure I looked foolish. But then, as always, the honor of obedience was totally worth it.

[Ryan] *I am continually amazed that I get to preach the gospel for a living. A couple of weeks ago I was giving a purity talk at a church. At the end of the evening I gave an opportunity for people to make two commitments. One was for purity, and the other was to Christ.*

For me, nothing compares to seeing people stand for Christ. In a crowd of a thousand people, if I see one person standing, it makes everything worthwhile. It'll always be hard to be away from home, to sleep in a strange bed, to miss seeing Laura and Lincoln each morning. But knowing I'll someday see one more person in heaven spurs me on to the next event.

No matter what response I get, I always thank God for giving me the privilege of sharing His message. He could have called someone else for this task, but He called me. And I'm honored.

155

When we live obediently, when we choose the narrow path, we're going to be wrecked. We're going to be uncomfortable, look foolish, and experience all kinds of hardship. And we might see no tangible result in our lifetimes. Sounds pretty grim, huh? But even if we see no evidence of our reward here on earth, it will certainly be a reality in heaven! And we obey not just for the reward but out of love for the One who has given us everything.

Think back to the disciples. They weren't honored in any way during their time on earth, but now they stand in history's hall of fame. And who knows—maybe they can look down from heaven today and see the multiplied effects of their obedience in the lives of believers all over the world!

We can all be wrecked the same way. How great is that?

Out of the Fish's Belly

— — —

In this moment, you might be in any of a variety of places spiritually and emotionally. Maybe you're buried under wreckage due to sinful choices you've made . . . maybe you're still digging yourself in deeper . . . maybe you're letting God change and heal your heart.

You might be reeling from some out-of-the-blue circumstance that you didn't cause and you can't control, possibly doubting and blaming God, possibly learning that He still loves you and has a purpose in everything that comes your way.

Or maybe you're struggling with God's challenge to seek after the honorable life of obedient wreckage.

Wherever we might be, what does it take to progress through our personal obstacle courses of challenges and then launch into a life of wrecked obedience? That obedient life is what we were made for. It's the natural human habitat, where we enjoy true fulfillment and purpose, even if sometimes with pain. How do we get there from here?

By God's amazing grace, the obedient life is within anyone's reach. No one is ever so "bad wrecked" that he or she can't become "good wrecked."

God can use any number of influences to turn us onto His path and guide us along it:

- He often uses a combination of His Word, other believers, and His Holy Spirit, as we've seen in the last chapter.
- He might send a crisis-inducing intervention or a friendly conversation.
- He's able to work inside our hearts and minds to remind and convict us of truths we already know.
- He can reveal new insights that lead to moments of unexplainable clarity, stirring us to make a change and showing us how to make it.
- He may allow the painful consequences of our sin to wake us up and wise us up.
- In the middle of nonsensical tragedy, we sometimes feel His comforting arms holding and protecting us.

Whatever His chosen method of the moment, we're not always receptive to it. Sometimes we resist stubbornly (maybe apathetically or maybe aggressively) for weeks,

months, or years before the impact of His message sinks
in. But in our experience, when God starts urging us
toward the next step of our journey toward Him, eventually we do one of two things: Either we dig in deeper to our
self-destruction and strain against God in a tug-of-war,
or we hand the rope to God and let Him lead us steadily
along the road—sometimes through forgiveness, sometimes through emotional recovery—to the obedient life.

Running Away

> The word of the LORD came to Jonah son of Amittai:
> "Go to the great city of Nineveh and preach against
> it, because its wickedness has come up before me."
> But Jonah ran away from the LORD and headed for
> Tarshish. He went down to Joppa, where he found
> a ship bound for that port. After paying the fare, he
> went aboard and sailed for Tarshish to flee from the
> LORD.[18]

159

Jonah. The mere mention of his name can make fish
sticks seem a little less appetizing. But more significantly,
his story can teach us a few principles about the way God
helps us get past our self-constructed obstacles and our
self-dug potholes and onto the journey to obedience.

His story gets off to a quick start. God told Jonah to
travel to idolatrous Nineveh and preach repentance.
Jonah said . . .

No.

What's more, he tried to run away. "Tried" is the operative word here. Even Jonah must have recognized the futility of trying to get away from an omnipresent God. But all of us delude ourselves sometimes and express our rebellion by trying to hide from God. Jonah disobeyed and tried to get away with it. His sin left him completely and utterly wrecked.

Nineveh was known throughout the world as a capital of corruption and evil. Jonah's Jewish upbringing trained him to respond, especially to their rampant idolatry, with self-righteous repulsion. In his mind, these degenerates who inhabited Nineveh were more than worthy of the worst God might pour out on them. Mercy was unthinkable. The world would be better without their putrid presence.

To Jonah, it seemed as though God had called him to walk into a spiritual leper colony. On top of his repulsion, he probably wasn't eager to go preaching judgment—*alone!*—in such a dangerous, God-hating place. He was terrified of terminal wreckage if he were to obey. So instead of embarking on the 3:15 to Nineveh, he scrambled onto the 1:57 to Tarshish, which would take him exactly the opposite direction.

A violent storm came up, the crew and passengers were sure they'd all drown, and Jonah finally got a clue. God was really mad; the storm was His way of getting Jonah's attention . . . in a big way!

Jonah didn't want innocent people to be wrecked because of his sin, so he told the others to throw him overboard in order to appease his God. As soon as they did, the waters stilled. That's when the giant fish slurped up Jonah.

Imagine Jonah's fear for his safety as the storm strengthened, and the sinking feeling in his stomach when he realized that the storm was *his fault*. Then the gut-wrenching decision to throw himself overboard, and finally that sinking feeling . . .

No doubt Jonah expected to die as he floundered in the dark, cold water. But next came a scene right out of *Jaws*. Maybe Jonah felt something bump his leg, saw a fin surge up out of the water. Then nothing for several seconds. (The bass strings section crescendos.) Next thing he knew, he was sliding down a slimy gullet into the fish's stomach—his residence for the next three days!

Now, if you ever find yourself in trouble, check out the prayer Jonah prayed in the fish's belly (see Jonah 2). Talk about panic! He was calling out to God for all he was worth. He'd come to terms with his true relationship to God. He knew he was sunk. And yet he knew enough to call out to the God who can keep someone alive inside a fish in the middle of a really big ocean.

And God answered. After three days the fish spit Jonah onto the shore. (Literally, the Bible says the fish vomited him up. Yeah, we know. Not very pretty.)

God spoke to Jonah again, repeating His previous instructions: "Go to the great city of Nineveh and proclaim to it the message I give you" (Jonah 3:2). Notice that, after Jonah had purposefully lost yardage because of his sin, God brought him right back to the line of scrimmage with exactly the same message. He said, in effect, "Now, where were we? Let's try that again." He didn't try to reason with Jonah or give him a pep talk. He simply allowed the hard lessons of Jonah's sojourn in disobedient wreckedness do the teaching. This time Jonah listened.

And his mission was a success! The Ninevites believed God, fasted, and went into mourning over their sins.

Jonah had to go through serious sin wreckage before he decided to obey God and bring the message of salvation to these "heathens." Even in his eventual obedience, Jonah was likely still disgusted, still afraid. But his fear of God outweighed his fear of and repulsion toward the Ninevites. Finally, a smart move. He would have avoided a lot of unnecessary pain if he'd obeyed God in the first place.

Now, let's take just a minute to consider one more lesson from this story. When God orchestrated the whole storm-and-fish thing, He was acting in love toward Jonah. That terrifying, slimy experience was definitely a wrecking one for Jonah. But it was nothing compared to the lifetime of desolate emptiness Jonah would have endured if God had allowed him to just sail away in disobedience.

When God intervenes in our lives with some form of wreckage to turn us away from sin, He's graciously protecting us from a lifetime of "successful" rebellion. He's trying to save us from a long, slow, soul-torturing wreck. And He's giving us another chance to reclaim the honor and joy of obedient wreckage.

Turning Around

When we pick up the story again in Jonah 4, we come to an interesting twist, after the Ninevites repented and God spared them from judgment.

> But Jonah was greatly displeased and became angry. He prayed to the LORD, "O LORD, is this not what I said when I was still at home? That is why I was so quick to flee to Tarshish. I knew that you are a gracious and compassionate God, slow to anger and abounding in love, a God who relents from sending calamity. Now, O LORD, take away my life, for it is better for me to die than to live."

> But the LORD replied, "Have you any right to be angry?"[19]

Despite the rejoicing of thousands who'd been spared from God's wrath, Jonah complained bitterly: "You're too nice, God. I can't believe You made me bring salvation to those pigs! Where's the justice? Besides, I can't get this fish slime off of me. Just kill me now, okay?"

So God set up a quick object lesson.

Jonah went out and sat down at a place east of the city. There he made himself a shelter, sat in its shade and waited to see what would happen to the city. Then the LORD God provided a vine and made it grow up over Jonah to give shade for his head to ease his discomfort, and Jonah was very happy about the vine. But at dawn the next day God provided a worm, which chewed the vine so that it withered. When the sun rose, God provided a scorching east wind, and the sun blazed on Jonah's head so that he grew faint. He wanted to die, and said, "It would be better for me to die than to live."

But God said to Jonah, "Do you have a right to be angry about the vine?"

"I do," he said. "I am angry enough to die."

But the LORD said, "You have been concerned about this vine, though you did not tend it or make it grow. It sprang up overnight and died overnight. But Nineveh has more than a hundred and twenty thousand people who cannot tell their right hand from their left, and many cattle as well. Should I not be concerned about that great city?"[20]

In this exchange, God revealed two aspects of His character: His desire to restore sinful people to Himself and

20 Jonah 4:5-11

His commitment to Jonah's (and our) spiritual growth. On the macro level, God loved the Ninevites and didn't want to destroy them. But also, on the micro level, notice His love in the way He handled Jonah. He wanted Jonah's heart and mind to become like God's—compassionate, accepting, forgiving. So He went out of his way to gently, patiently teach Jonah about His compassion.

In our turnarounds, God accomplishes multiple loving purposes, all at the same time. Through our obedience, He makes life-changing differences in the lives of those we serve. And He draws us, the servants, closer to Himself and His character. Christlikeness is the best gift He could ever give us, whether we recognize it or not.

165

What about Us?

There's really only one way to obey God's call completely. But we can be quite creative in our methods for disobeying. We can rebel by running. Or we can saunter casually away from our task. (*Maybe He won't notice.*) And sometimes we just freeze up and get stuck.

Our motives can be as varied as our methods. Fear and trembling, self-righteous revulsion, discomfort, and apathy are just a few. But in every situation, no matter what the variations on the theme, we end up making a choice between yes and no, between obedience and disobedience. And though we try to rationalize rebellion, there's no way to escape God.

[Toben] *During my season of running, God's will for me was that I get healthy, both emotionally and physically. My mental illness, my inactivity (I spent a lot of time in bed and on the couch), and my drinking were working together to bring destruction to myself. And eventually destruction to the things and people I held most dear.*

I knew that what He had planned for me was much better than my present misery and wreckage. But for some reason that didn't connect with me, and I stayed in rebellion. Spiritual warfare inside me was a big reason for my relapse into alcoholism, and part of my ongoing struggle. I didn't want to hear God's voice—or anyone else's, for that matter. I guess you could say that alcohol was the giant fish that swallowed me. But instead of praying, I just wallowed. And Satan couldn't have been happier!

After a while, God used friends and family in a dramatic way to get my attention, and it worked. I got help. I went to a psychologist, a psychiatrist, a family doctor, AA meetings, and church. It gradually became clear to me, after I started taking care of my head, my heart, my body, and my soul, that I was doing exactly what God had asked me to do—He wanted me to be healthy and whole; I was finally on His path.

That first, foundational task was strategic. My health was a necessary prerequisite before I could obey in other important ways, like becoming the best husband and father I can be. Only when I'm healthy am I able to invest everything in my family and stick around long enough to see my girls grow up.

I kick myself sometimes for running so far from God. God

*provided all kinds of opportunities for me to turn back to Him,
to health, to my family. I can remember each chance I had for
change. And I remember walking right past them. I could have
saved myself and my loved ones a lot of scars by just leaning
into my pain and learning from it instead of desperately avoiding it.*

*Fast-forward a couple of years. . . . God is still working on
me. I'm closer to being on target, less likely to shoot off into
oblivion. I can feel God nudging me closer to the center of His
will all the time. I've never felt better—physically, emotionally,
and spiritually. My once-damaged relationships are being
restored beyond my hopes and dreams. Joanne and the girls
have become the lights of my life, the center of my universe.*

*I just wish I had taken the shortcut Jesus offered instead of
going the long way around.*

Have you ever run away from God's calling, from something you thought would wreck you? Are you running now?
Has a gentle nudge toward obedience—or a flashing neon
billboard—petrified you into fearful inactivity? Whether
you've run or are simply frozen, how has the wreckage of
your disobedience shown up? Have you been swallowed
whole by an unhealthy relationship, an addiction, materialism . . . ? Is something small and subtle gnawing at you
from the inside, eroding your peace of mind?

Here's the thing to do: Turn around and *lean into* whatever is causing you pain. In other words, take active measures to engage your pain. Sit with it, journal about it, talk

to a trusted friend about it. Whatever is the most effective way for you to learn from your pain . . . just do it.

Keep in mind, too, that Jesus is lovingly relentless. He doesn't abandon His call on you. In the end, God didn't tell Jonah, "I guess you've suffered enough, so cancel what I said. Forget Nineveh. Just go on back home." God calls you to obedience, and then He steadfastly keeps calling—using a little wreckage here and there, if necessary—until you accept it.

That might be bad news to some of us. We have it in the back of our heads that if we run far enough or fast enough, we'll get away from God's life-wrecking mission.

Bogus. And it's a good thing too. Even if we could escape, would we really *want* to live our lives running from God?

Leaning Into It

[Ryan] *In the past five years I've had to make two big career decisions. The first was the decision to get into a speaking and writing ministry. I had successfully run an IT department, and many people tried to steer me away from ministry, toward another "real" job in IT. I probably could have started a lucrative career that way. But I just knew in my heart that my passion wasn't in that kind of work; I wasn't called to be a computer technician, no matter how many late-night commercials told me otherwise.*

The second major decision was to start KOR Ministries. KOR started out as a side project ministering to the skate—meaning skateboard—community. I helped lead a couple of skate mission trips but never considered taking it further. My speaking and writing career was taking off, and it was rewarding. I was speaking about a hundred times a year, and I had written a book a year for three straight years. Why would I add anything else to my already busy schedule? But I was feeling a clear call from the Lord to something more. More of what, I didn't know. At that time an old friend contacted me and asked if I'd ever considered going into radio. I smiled and thought, Okay Lord, I hear you.

You see, I hadn't been thinking about radio, but I had been thinking about podcasting, which would allow me more freedom. I could record and post shows at will. I was newly married and didn't want to be on the road one hundred dates a year; podcasting looked like a promising alternative. I began turning KOR into a full-fledged ministry.

But fewer speaking dates meant less money. Less money doesn't work very well in Orange County. About that time I was invited to speak in Colorado Springs.

In the early nineties I had lived outside the Springs and just didn't think it was for me. I'd never thought of moving there. I loved Orange County. I loved my friends, the beach, the food, the lifestyle, my church, and my apartment with its ocean view.

Besides my attraction to the OC, there was my dislike of CO. I'm not a fan of the cold—unless it involves skiing—and I certainly didn't want to live in the snow.

Still, two thoughts ran through my mind as Laura and I

traveled to Colorado Springs. First, the average home price in the OC had blown past $700,000, and my decreasing ministry salary made home ownership unlikely. And second, a little voice from the Lord kept saying, "Just think about it. Just open your eyes to new possibilities."

The plane landed and I opened my eyes.

Laura and I looked around at the options available to us, and we consciously, actively listened to the Lord. Soon I was convinced that Colorado was where God was leading us, but I never expected Laura to go for it. Laura had lived within sight of the ocean almost since birth, and she was surfing about four days a week. Her entire family lived there—four brothers, four sisters-in-law, twelve nieces and nephews, her parents, her grandma, and various uncles, aunts, and cousins—not to mention her countless friends.

So I told the Lord, "Okay, my eyes are open, but you have to convince my brand-new wife to leave the ocean and her family to move to the Rockies, the Frozen Empire." We were both apprehensive. Finally, we made a deal that we would try it out for six months, and if either of us hated it, we'd move back to California.

I fully expected Laura to take advantage of the opt-out clause at her first opportunity, but we've been here almost two years, and we expect to raise a family here. We've fallen in love with Colorado Springs. We've made new friends, the Lord led us to a great church, and our ministry has taken off in ways we never imagined.

Was it scary? Yes. But God had been faithful in leading us to each other, and now He was leading us here.

As much as we love it here, we'll go anywhere else He might send us. Both of us firmly believe that God calls us to the best life, if not necessarily an easy one.

"Good wrecked" is all about saying yes to God. It's about trusting Him to see us through the fears and challenges that come along with obedience. It's about using our freedom to work with God, when we could choose to work against Him.

All kinds of good things come out of our obedient wreckage. We gain assurance that we're doing the right thing. We honor and glorify God. We learn about ourselves. We learn about dependence on God. And we learn what we're capable of even when we're afraid.

Leaning into the wreckage is a stretch, to be sure. But in reality, we're fortunate to be pushed and tested. We're blessed in the hard lessons that teach us faith. And in the future, we'll be reassured by memories of God's love and faithfulness in our present-day hardships.

Ultimately, leaning into and learning from our wrecked lives transforms our very character, shaping us into the people God has always meant us to be. We learn to welcome our challenges when we realize that we're eternally better off wrecking our lives by obedience.

U-Turns

Wherever you find yourself at the moment, don't give up. Are you wrecked because of bad choices? There's no point

RYAN DOBSON AND TOBEN HEIM

in beating yourself up. God doesn't give extra credit for self-flagellation. He *does* give credit for turning around; we serve a God who allows U-turns. When you admit your mess-ups and ask God to help you change, He promises to forgive you and heal you.

It's easy, once we begin the journey away from our bad choices, to shut them into the past and never think about them again. That's natural; no one wants to dwell on pain. But maybe grab a piece of paper and write a few lessons you learned. Then tuck it away. Or sit down with a trusted friend and talk it through. Just don't lose the opportunity to learn, to redeem a bad situation for all its worth.

Are you wrecked by difficult circumstances you didn't cause? Avoid the temptation to numb out. Face reality with courage from God. Denial won't make the problem disappear. Welcome the chance to reveal and refine your character; then you can deal with your circumstances head-on.

Are you suffering because of good and obedient choices you've made? Take heart. You're following in some mighty impressive footprints, too many to list here. Be honest about your pain—especially with God—but beware of the trap of excessive self-pity.

And please—*please!*—don't try to go through anything alone. God didn't design us to fly solo through life's storms. We hope you're involved in a solid, Bible-believing church with people ready to jump in with prayer, encouragement, and support. Or that you'll find one soon. And that along the way, God will provide friends to walk beside you.

Inviting others into our wreckage can be embarrassing. But remember: Everyone else has their wrecks in their lives too. Take a chance and let someone in.

You need a cheerleader—not the bubbly kind in a short skirt—who'll be there for you. In AA this person's called a sponsor. Get yourself an "obedience sponsor" who'll take your calls anytime, who'll commit to pray for you, encourage you, and comfort you. If no one comes to mind, one of your pastors or other church leaders might know someone who would jump at the chance.

As you're developing community with other people, look for companionship in the Bible as well. It's full of people who made the right decisions and got kicked in the teeth for it. You're not alone.

And one more thing: Once you've leaned into and learned from your own struggle, be ready to help wrecked people around you. To fully redeem your wrecked experience, you need to share your hope and strength with others. Pray for God to bring the right people across your path; maybe you'll get the chance to bless the socks off someone.

In all your wrecks, know that Christ is there with you, as He has been with countless others. Be confident, even when you're most broken, that God will bring glory and good out of your suffering—glory for Him and good for you.

When your life crashes and burns, rest assured that it's infinitely better to be wrecked in the palm of His hand than to be "safe" anywhere else.

Acknowledgments

I have many people to thank. First I want to thank and give special recognition to my friend Toben. It was you who brought the concept of this book to me and helped to coax it out of me. It was difficult to revisit times past, but your friendship and support allowed me to be vulnerable and open in a way I wasn't able to be on my own. I can't thank you enough for the writes, rewrites, and re-rewrites it took to finish this book. I have been honored and blessed to have worked with you. But I am more honored and more blessed to have you as a friend. Thanks for having my back.

Many times it seemed as if this book wasn't going to see the light of day. I want to thank Doug Knox and Tyndale for believing in us and seeing the value in our message. Thanks also to Stephanie Voiland for putting this puzzle together. The final picture really is amazing. God bless you all.

—R. D.

I'd like to thank Stephanie Voiland for all the work she put into this project. I'd like to thank my friend Ryan for jumping into this project with me and bringing his fresh ideas and so many stories to these pages. Ryan, I know it was a difficult and long road to bring this book into being, but the journey was made easier because we got to walk the path together.

I'd like to thank the people who really taught me the lessons included in these pages: Chuck and Kay Friedenstein, for their steadfast love and support and encouragement; Jim and Susan Hancock, who were there with unconditional love for me when I crashed and burned; Jen and Jay Howver, who put a lot on the line to push me to get the help I needed. I credit you all with saving my life. Finally I want to thank Joanne, Audrey, and Emma—you are my greatest joys. Thanks for giving me those few hours each morning to write this thing. Thanks for your hugs and kisses and other simple expressions of love. And most of all, thanks for being the embodiment of grace. I love you all dearly.

—T. H.

About the Authors

"If I could be doing anything in the world, it would be this."

With the conviction that comes from knowing your purpose—and loving every minute of it—Ryan Dobson passionately pursues his calling in Christ. From his books to his podcast to his speaking engagements, Ryan uses every opportunity to call people out of the moral relativism in today's society and into the ultimate adventure of following Christ.

Born in 1970, Ryan grew up as the second of two children of famous family counselor, author, and radio host James Dobson. While many pushed him to follow in his father's footsteps, Ryan took the time to explore his own gifts while trusting in Jesus as his guide. After graduating from college, Ryan found that his natural talent for public speaking, combined with his passion for youth, soon opened countless doors.

Ryan traveled extensively for years, challenging youth at music festivals, concert tours, youth camps, and conferences. Drawing from his experiences talking firsthand to teenagers and young adults, he wrote his first book, *Be Intolerant*, in 2003. This wake-up call warned young Christians not to fall for the lies of a relativistic, postmodern society. Described by *Publishers Weekly* as having "a colloquial style with all the subtlety of a two-by-four to the side of the head," it quickly rose up the sales charts, followed by two more best sellers: *To Die For* and *To Live For.*

Behind the scenes, Ryan has been developing his own base—KOR World Ministries, with the purpose of building passion and identity in followers of Christ (KORWorldMinistries.com). He produces KORKast, a podcast that challenges listeners in the way they interact with culture. He also continues to speak, write, and lead short-term mission trips and men's retreats.

Ryan has a bachelor's degree in communication studies from Biola University. He lives in Colorado with his wife, Laura, and their son, Lincoln.

Toben Heim is the coauthor with his wife, Joanne, of *Happily Ever After: A Real Life Look at Your First Year of Marriage . . . and Beyond, www.mosaixstudy.com/community, www.mosaixstudy.com/men&women,* and *What's Your Story? An Interactive Guide to Building Authentic Relationships.*

Toben and Joanne were high school sweethearts, and he proposed the night before she graduated from high school. They attended Whitworth College in Spokane, Washington, and got married in 1991. Toben graduated in 1993 with a degree in communication studies and lots of experience in all-night student government meetings as the vice president of the student body.

After a summer in Paris wandering the city and sitting at cafés for hours, the Heims moved to Colorado, where Toben began his career as a road rep for NavPress Publishing Group, traveling to the Northeast and racking up frequent flier miles while visiting bookstores and discovering great Cajun food in New Jersey (who knew?). During the next ten years he became a dad (twice!—to two beautiful girls, Audrey and Emma), the sales and marketing director, and eventually the publisher for *The Message*.

By 2003 the Heims couldn't resist the call of the ocean and moved to Southern California, where Toben worked for Youth Specialties.

In 2006 the Heims moved back to Denver to live near family. Toben now runs his own marketing and publishing consulting firm and drives the carpool each day.

Books by RYAN DOBSON

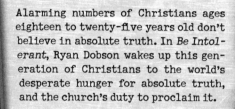

Alarming numbers of Christians ages eighteen to twenty-five years old don't believe in absolute truth. In *Be Intolerant*, Ryan Dobson wakes up this generation of Christians to the world's desperate hunger for absolute truth, and the church's duty to proclaim it.

If you have nothing worth dying for, you have nothing worth living for. Ryan Dobson passionately demonstrates what it means to die to self and gives clear guidance for making life-or-death choices every day.

Building on the call to die to self in *To Die For*, Ryan Dobson shows you how to experience the thrill of coming alive. *To Live For* challenges you to pursue a life that's raw and real—and totally sold-out for Jesus.

Available everywhere books are sold.

CP0179